Zionism: A Very Short Introduction

VERY SHORT INTRODUCTIONS are for anyone wanting a stimulating and accessible way into a new subject. They are written by experts, and have been translated into more than 40 different languages.

The series began in 1995, and now covers a wide variety of topics in every discipline. The VSI library now contains over 450 volumes—a Very Short Introduction to everything from Indian philosophy to psychology and American history and relativity—and continues to grow in every subject area.

Very Short Introductions available now:

Available soon:

For more information visit our web site

www.oup.com/vsi/

Michael Stanislawski

ZIONISM

A Very Short Introduction

OXFORD
UNIVERSITY PRESS

OXFORD

UNIVERSITY PRESS

Oxford University Press is a department of the University of Oxford.
It furthers the University's objective of excellence in research, scholarship,
and education by publishing worldwide. Oxford is a registered trade mark of
Oxford University Press in the UK and certain other countries.

Published in the United States of America by Oxford University Press
198 Madison Avenue, New York, NY 10016, United States of America.

© Oxford University Press 2017

Library of Congress Cataloging-in-Publication Data

Names: Stanislawski, Michael, 1952- author.
Title: Zionism : a very short introduction / Michael Stanislawski.
Description: New York : Oxford University Press, 2017. |
Series: Very short introductions | Includes bibliographical references and index.
Identifiers: LCCN 2016028235| ISBN 9780199766048 (paperback) |
ISBN 9780199908554 (ebook updf) | ISBN 9780190625207 (online resource)
Subjects: LCSH: Zionism—History. | BISAC: HISTORY / Jewish.
Classification: LCC DS149 .S6585 2016 | DDC 320.54095694—dc23 LC record
available at https://lccn.loc.gov/2016028235

MIX
Paper
FSC   FSC® C183721

Printed by Integrated Books International, United States of America
on acid-free paper

In memory of Sumner Z. Kaplan

Contents

Zionism

List of illustrations

Chapter 1
The Jews: Religion or Nation?

Zionism—the nationalist movement calling for the establishment and support of an independent state for the Jewish people in its ancient homeland—is today one of the most controversial ideologies in the world. Its supporters see it as the national liberation movement of the Jewish people that came to fruition in the creation of the State of Israel in 1948. Its opponents regard it as one of the last forms of colonial oppression in the world today, defined by Israel's occupation of the West Bank and its millions of Palestinian residents in the name of a racist ideology increasingly turning Israel into an apartheid state.

As can easily be imagined, one result of this controversy is a highly politicized historical literature, with virtually all works on the subject espousing either of those positions or a variation thereof. Objectivity has ceased to be a goal not only of popular writing on the subject but also of scholarship, and the line between intellectual engagement and political activism hardly exists today.

What this book attempts to do, therefore, is not to produce an impossible-to-achieve objective account of its subject, but to produce instead one defined by a highly self-conscious scholarly detachment, not promoting any particular political position on Zionism, either in its favor or opposed to it. Proponents both of

Zionism and of anti-Zionism might well argue that this goal is at best elusive, at worst disingenuous. It will be up to the reader to decide whether the aim of detachment has been achieved.

Where to start is itself the object of scholarly and polemical controversy. Many, if not most, Zionists today regard Zionism as a natural continuation of two millennia of Jewish attachment to the Land of Israel and aspiration to return there in the End of Days. According to this view, Jews prayed daily through the millennia for the restoration of a Jewish homeland in Palestine, and this hope was realized dramatically, and, for some, miraculously, in the establishment of the State of Israel in 1948.

What this common point of view misunderstands is that the Zionist movement, founded in the late nineteenth century under highly specific and contingent circumstances, was in fact a rejection of that age-old desire for the Jews to return to the Land of Israel, and not its linear fulfillment. This was, quite simply, because that traditional "yearning for Zion" was tied inexorably to the belief in the advent of a messiah chosen and anointed by God—and by God alone—who would then initiate the "ingathering of the exiles" (i.e., the return to Zion of all the Jews in the world) and the rebuilding of the Temple in Jerusalem. In most of its versions, Jewish messianism also—and crucially—entailed an end to earthly existence as we know it. At the end of time, the redemption of the Jewish people would go hand in hand with an end not only to history but to the natural order of the cosmos. As the Book of Isaiah so beautifully put it, "Nation shall not lift up sword against nation, neither shall they learn war anymore," and "the wolf shall dwell with the lamb, and the leopard shall lie down with the young goat, and the calf and the lion and the fattened calf together; and a little child shall lead them."

This messianic vision did lead some Jews throughout history to declare that the end of days was nigh and the actual messiah had indeed arrived: the two most famous manifestations of this belief were Christianity and the rather less well-known late seventeenth-century movement following Sabbetai Zevi, a Jew from the Ottoman Empire who eventually converted to Islam rather than face death. But in between Jesus and Sabbetai Zevi there were many other "false messiahs," and so the rabbinic leadership of the Jews worldwide declared that although the messianic belief and its call for the Jews to return to the Holy Land was a cardinal doctrine of Judaism, they decried any apocalyptic version of that belief: Jews were forbidden to "advance the end" or even to calculate it. The messiah would be chosen by God on God's good time, and any activism among human beings to intervene in this process was heresy, to be condemned and punished.

The founders of Zionism rebelled fundamentally and viscerally against the political quietism which was the corollary of this messianic belief. They demanded that Jews take matters into their own hands to liberate themselves, not to wait for God (in whom many—quite crucially—no longer believed) to return the Jews to "Zion" to create a Jewish homeland there. In the sharpest contrast to the suspension of the natural order of existence in the messianic age articulated by Isaiah, Zionism from the start called for the "normalization" of the Jewish people: that the Jews treat themselves, and be treated by the rest of the world, like all other nations inhabiting the globe in the here and now.

The basic premise of this ideology was that the Jews constitute a nation, and not a religion—a redefinition of Jewishness that resulted from a broader ideological innovation in Jewish history: the creation of modern Jewish nationalism. Indeed, in most ways Zionism followed the common pattern of modern nationalist movements, which began in the early nineteenth century in Western and Central Europe and then spread into Eastern Europe in the middle and late nineteenth century. These began as ideologies of cultural renaissance among small groups of intellectuals and writers who were heavily influenced by the ideas

of philosophers such as J. G. Herder and J. G. Fichte, who argued
that humanity was fundamentally divided into distinct "nations,"
each of which had a unique history, culture, and "national spirit"
(*Volksgeist* in German). Thus, the word "nation," which previously
had a very loose meaning that could apply to essentially any group
of people united by some common bond (one spoke, for example,
of the "nation of students"), now acquired a highly specific and
exclusive meaning: every person's primary identification was
as a member of his or her nation, rather than other forms of
self-definition or loyalty—religious, regional, local, even familial.
This superseding national identity required, among other things,
a continuous common history (invented by nationalist historians),
led by national heroes reaching back to antiquity, and a "national
language" which had to replace previous modes of communication,
now derogated as dialects which had to be eliminated. In due
course, crucial to the new nationalisms was the insistence that
each nation required political sovereignty—preferably, complete
independence—in clearly demarcated territories that belonged in
a biological manner to that nation and that nation alone, but had
in whole or in part been taken away from it by foreign occupiers,
from which it had to be liberated.

However, the translation of this last plank of the new notion of
nationhood into reality was extremely problematic, since most
states in Europe—and elsewhere, as nationalism spread to the
rest of the world—were not organized either demographically
or politically along such exclusive "national" lines but instead
in states in which members of different ethnic and religious
groups lived side by side in cities, towns, and villages, either
peaceably or in an often tense but still stable modus vivendi.
As the rise of the new nationalisms continued, however, this
situation was viewed as inherently unnatural, unjust, and
oppressive. At best, people who did not belong to one's nation
could be tolerated as "minority" populations, but only on the
condition that they recognize that they were essentially
strangers in a foreign land.

While for the most part Zionism followed this common pattern of modern nationalisms, it also diverged from it in crucial ways. First, since antiquity the Jews had described themselves, and had been defined by others, as a "people" or a "nation," even though the latter term was understood in a different way from its later nationalist usage. Thus, the Hebrew Bible uses three words to convey the concepts of Jewish peoplehood or nationality: *am*, *goy*, and *leom*. It is not at all clear what the difference was, if any, between these terms for the Biblical authors, but over the course of time the most common appellation for the Jews as a group became *am yisrael*, the people of Israel. With the invention of modern Jewish nationalism in the middle and late nineteenth century, however, the third and least common Biblical term—*leom*—came to be used as the basis for the Hebrew versions of the new European conceptions of "nation," "nationhood," and "nationalism," so as not to confuse them with the more typical pre-nineteenth-century terms.

Perhaps an example from the part of the world in which modern Jewish nationalism was invented—the former Russian Empire—will help clarify this rather complex point. Until the twentieth century, the nation now known as Belarusians did not exist: the vast majority of the population of this territory (now the country Belarus) were peasants who practiced Eastern Orthodox Christianity and spoke an East Slavic dialect (or, more precisely, a range of dialects) close to, but distinct from, Russian and Ukrainian. Their primary modes of self-identification were their religion, their places of origins, and their families or clans. They did not think of themselves as a "nation" in any sense of the term. It was only with the invention of modern Belarusian nationalism in the late nineteenth and early twentieth century on the part of a small group of intellectuals that this nation came into existence, and then was—paradoxically—aided enormously by the supposedly supranational, and indeed antinationalist, Soviet state. By now, Belarusians believe that they are, and always have been, a distinct nation with a distinct history, national language, and literature going back to antiquity.

In brief, unlike the Belarusians, Jews had thought of themselves, and had been thought of by others, as a "nation" for millennia, but what that term signified changed radically in the wake of modern nationalism.

The Jews differed fundamentally from other newly defined (or newly invented) nations for two other critical reasons. First, for thousands of years the word "Jew" also referred to someone who adhered to and practiced (what we now call) Judaism—a distinct system of religious beliefs, laws, and customs, and neither Jews nor non-Jews saw any problem in a group being defined in both national and religious terms. It was only in the Enlightenment of the late seventeenth and the eighteenth centuries that the separation between these two concepts and these two realms of life was introduced: the political (viewed as belonging to the public realm) and the religious (viewed as belonging to private realm); as a result, the debate began over whether to define the Jews exclusively as a nation or as a religious group.

Secondly, unlike the example of the Belarusians, the Jews did not live as the majority population of any territory, but rather as minority populations of countries virtually throughout the globe. To be sure, no one denied that the Jews had had a national homeland in antiquity (such a claim would wait for so-called post-Zionist and anti-Zionist scholars in the late twentieth century). This homeland was known variously as Judea, Palestine, the Holy Land, the Land of Israel—from which the vast majority of the Jews had been exiled by the Romans in 70 CE. While a small remnant remained there throughout the ages, they constituted a small percentage both of the population of what came to be known as "Palestine" and of the Jewish population throughout the world. Crucially, despite this demographic reality, the memory of the Holy Land and its centrality to Judaism and the Jewish people was retained through the ages, recalled in daily and festival liturgies that prayed for God to restore the Jews to the Holy Land at the end of history, in the messianic age. Best known is the prayer "Next year in Jerusalem," pronounced at the end of the Passover Seder or as the concluding prayer of Yom Kippur. But this profound belief in the ultimate return of the Jews to the Land of Israel had far more day-to-day ramifications: it is included numerous times in the daily liturgy of all Jewish rites around the world, in the morning, afternoon, and evening prayers, and in the grace after meals. To cite a minor but evocative example, although the Jews lived in parts of the world in which the weather, and hence the agricultural cycle, was far different from that of Palestine, they continued to pray for propitious weather to sustain successful agriculture in Palestine according to the planting and harvest seasons there. Moreover, it became a practice in many parts of the Jewish world for Jews to be buried with a small sack of earth from the Land of Israel in their coffins—a symbolic gesture with profound eschatological import.

The issue of Jews actually immigrating to Palestine through the centuries was immensely complicated by the doctrinal strictures of the messianic belief in Judaism as it came to be articulated through the centuries. Nonetheless, a small number of Jews did immigrate to Palestine throughout the centuries, at times out of messianic expectations but more often to reside and study in its holy cities, to fulfill commandments that applied solely to the Holy Land, and to be buried in its holy soil.

In highly complex and often paradoxical ways, Zionism drew on this reservoir of thousands of years of Jewish longing for a return to the Land of Israel. But, once more, the alpha and omega of its ideology was its redefinition of the Jews as a nation like all other nations. And this redefinition not only preceded the emergence of Zionism per se but led as well to the formation of other forms of modern Jewish nationalism that rejected out of hand the return of the Jews to Palestine, calling instead for their political reinvigoration in the Diaspora.

Despite these basic and often vituperative differences, all ideologies of modern Jewish nationalism proceeded from, and shared, two basic assumptions beyond the fact the Jews constituted a "nation" in the new sense of the term: first, that the goal of "emancipation"—the attainment of equal rights—acquired first by the Jews of France in 1790 and 1791 and then struggled for by Jews throughout the rest of Europe for most of the nineteenth century—was not only unattainable and hence illusory but, on an even more basic level, fundamentally flawed, since emancipation and integration into other nation-states contradicted the very notion that the Jews constituted a nation of their own. Thus, while both the nationalists and the supporters of emancipation explicitly accepted the separation between nation and religion introduced by the Enlightenment, each side came to the exact opposite conclusion based on that distinction.

Secondly, this view intersected in a complex way with the fact that most modern Jewish nationalists rejected the millennia-old religious beliefs and traditions of the Jews, including (for many, though not all) the belief in God. These beliefs and traditions, the new Jewish nationalists claimed, had been superseded by the discoveries of science, the Enlightenment, Darwin (and for the socialists, Marx)—in short, by modernity itself. The only rational conclusion, therefore, was that the liberation of the Jews was their own responsibility, not that of a (probably nonexistent) God. Thus, Zionists and the other Jewish nationalists also rejected the new religious movements that had emerged in Western and Central European Jewry in the nineteenth century: the Reform, Positive-Historical, and Neo-Orthodox movements all shared the belief, for example, that the Jews in Germany were Germans of the Mosaic faith, parallel to Germans of the Catholic or Protestant faiths, and so too should Jews be considered in every country in the world, as the march of civilization progressed and as the Jews would be emancipated as equal citizens of all modern states. Thus, to most Jews in Western Europe, it was Judaism itself that commanded them to remain where they were, and to act as loyal subjects of the state in which they lived.

The problem was that not all states, even in Western Europe, were prepared to treat the Jews as members of their own national community separated only by religious creed, and hence to emancipate the Jews as equal citizens. Indeed, very soon after the invention of modern Jewish nationalism there emerged a new form of Jew hatred: racially based anti-Semitism, first appearing in both France and Germany. But here one must be very precise about chronology: the all-too-frequent claim that modern Jewish nationalism was born in response to anti-Semitism or to the outbreak of violent attacks ("pogroms") against the Jews which began in the Russian Empire in 1881–82 is quite simply wrong: the first expressions of this new ideology were published well before the spread of the new anti-Semitic ideology and before the pogroms of the early 1880s. This is not to deny that the pogroms and the spread of anti-Semitic ideology convinced many Jews of the veracity of the modern nationalist, including the Zionist, solutions to the "Jewish problem." But once more, it is essential to understand that the fundamental cause of the emergence of modern Jewish nationalism was the rise, on the part of Jews themselves, of new ideologies that applied the basic tenets of modern nationalism to the Jews, and not a response to persecution.

Indeed, the rise of anti-Semitism even in its most virulent forms did not lead the vast majority of Jews worldwide to abandon their belief in Judaism as a religious faith, whether in its traditional or modernist versions, or their belief that legal emancipation—and its corollary of upward economic and social mobility—would solve the problem of the Jews. Thus, even in the face of the rise of anti-Semitism, for most of its history Zionism remained a distinctly minority view in Jewish communities around the world, opposed by the vast majority of rabbinic and lay leaders. This situation changed only after the murder of six million Jews in the Holocaust, when the need for an independent Jewish state to serve as a safe haven for Jews became not only widespread but central to Jewish consciousness throughout the world.

But this is putting the cart well before the horse: we must return to the mid-nineteenth century to witness the birth first of modern Jewish nationalism and then, in 1897, of its most important and long-lived offshoot, the Zionist movement.

Chapter 2
Modern Jewish nationalism, 1872–1897

In almost all textbooks on modern Jewish history or on Zionism itself, a good deal of attention is paid to so-called precursors, forerunners, or harbingers of Zionism, a small number of men (and one famous woman, George Eliot) in the mid-nineteenth century who advocated the return of the Jews to Palestine and thus presaged the advent of the Zionist movement.

But the very idea of "precursors," "forerunners," or "harbingers" of any movement or ideology is profoundly problematic conceptually: put most simply, it accepts—almost entirely unconsciously—the inevitability of the emergence of a given movement or ideology and then anachronistically seeks out figures who preached ideas similar to the movements or ideologies that actually emerged. This retrojection ignores or distorts the vast differences between these earlier ideas and those that defined the ideologies or movements they allegedly presaged. In this process, the thorniest issue of historical interpretation—cause and effect—is turned on its head and misrepresented. Thus, to have any meaning, an authentic "forerunner," "precursor," or "harbinger" of any movement must—by definition—have had influence on the actual historical, flesh-and-blood movements they are identified with. Crucial for the case of Zionism is that there was *no* such influence, not even a scintilla of cause and effect.

The three most often cited "forerunners of Zionism" were two rabbis, Zvi Hirsch Kalischer and Yehuda Solomon Alkalai, and one socialist thinker, Moses Hess. These men adduced interesting (and contradictory) arguments in favor of a return of the Jews to Palestine, but they had virtually no audience during their lifetimes and—crucially—were unknown to the actual inventors of modern Jewish nationalism and of Zionism whom we shall presently encounter. Moreover, had the latter ever read the writings of Rabbis Kalischer and Alkalai, they would have rejected the very basis of their traditionalist religious and largely mystical worldviews. Similarly, none of the actual founders of Zionism had ever heard of or read Moses Hess's *Rome and Jerusalem* before they enunciated their own ideas; and once more, had they read his book, they would have rejected its highly idiosyncratic blend of socialism and belief in the necessity of preserving Orthodox Judaism as the basis of the future Jewish state in Palestine until the advent of the socialist utopia.

It was only *after* the creation of Zionism that these "precursors" were identified and summoned, as it were, as witnesses for the defense, and particularly on the part of adherents of particular brands of Zionism. Thus, after the creation of the Orthodox Zionist movement, Mizrachi, in 1902, its beleaguered leaders, attacked by the vast majority of traditionalist and Orthodox rabbis the world over, searched for authorities who they could claim supported their point of view. To their delight, they then uncovered the writings of Rabbis Kalischer and Alkalai, ostensibly providing rabbinic imprimatur for their alleged heterodoxy. The fact that the worldviews of these rabbis were radically different both from each other's and from the fundamental outlook of the Mizrachi movement was conveniently ignored. In precisely the same manner, after the creation of socialist Zionist movements beginning in 1899, Moses Hess was retroactively anointed as a precursor to these ideologies, since he was both a socialist and had called for the return of the Jews to Palestine—again, conveniently ignoring the fact that virtually no one read his book when it was published and that it was based on highly peculiar views that were all but totally irreconcilable with those of the various socialist Zionist movements that existed in reality.

The true historical invention of modern Jewish nationalism, and then Zionism, did not have any "precursors" but was the result of an internal development within the Jewish Enlightenment movement known as the Haskalah. That movement began in Germany in the mid-eighteenth century, especially under the aegis of Moses Mendelssohn, one of the most formidable philosophers of his age. Mendelssohn—joining in and helping to refine the philosophical distinction between nationhood and religion—argued forcefully for the latter definition of the Jews: they were members of a religion known as Judaism, which, in his rather idiosyncratic view, had no theological doctrines unique to it and distinct from the "natural religion" innate in all human beings through Reason. Jews were nonetheless obliged to follow the commandments and laws of Judaism, for one simple reason: God had commanded them, and them alone, to do so. As a devout Jew, Mendelssohn retained a firm belief in the traditional messianic promise made to the Jews by God, but this did not interfere with his basic definition of the Jews as members of a religious faith who had to be tolerated, like all other religious communities, in a modern free state.

This fundamental teaching of Mendelssohn retained its centrality in the Jewish Enlightenment movement in Central Europe after Mendelssohn's death, but as it spread to Eastern Europe, it encountered a far different reality: here lived the vast majority of the world's Jews (around one million in the late eighteenth century) in multinational empires in which the Jews were both legally defined and saw themselves as distinct ethnic as well as religious communities. They lived largely in densely populated communities in cities and smaller market towns, where they constituted a substantial percentage (and sometimes even the majority) of the population. In the Russian Empire, where most of the Jews lived, the concept of "citizen" in the modern (i.e., post–French Revolution) sense simply did not exist: the population—whether nobles, clergy, peasants, or members of the urban groups to which the Jews were legally assigned—were subjects of autocratic monarchs who granted privileges at their whim, rather than acknowledging any concept of inherent or innate rights, even (as in the West) for the aristocracy or clergy. Hence, the very ideas of "emancipation" and "equal rights" were fundamentally foreign to the basic legal political structures of the Russian state. (In the Russian-controlled Kingdom of Poland the Jews were formally emancipated in 1862, but this had almost no effect in real life.) In the Habsburg Empire, which acquired the area of the former Polish-Lithuanian Commonwealth known as Galicia, which included hundreds of thousands of (largely impoverished) Jews, the legacy of Roman law was far more influential, and hence there did exist notions of innate rights; nonetheless, the possibility of legal emancipation for the Jews (or for other so-called minority groups) was simply not conceivable until the rise of modern nationalism in the mid-nineteenth century.

Nonetheless, the ideologies of the Jewish Enlightenment movement as it spread to Galicia and then reached its apogee in the Russian-dominated lands, continued to hold—as did the so-called Westernizers among the Russian intelligentsia—that the tide of history was in favor of the transformation of Russia along the lines of the West, and thus not only would the Jews eventually attain emancipation on the French model, but they (like the Russians themselves) had to prove themselves worthy of such emancipation by modernizing themselves. For the Jews this meant rejecting their fundamental intellectual presupposition that Truth was contained in, and ascertainable solely through, study of the Bible and its explication in the Talmud. Rather, the Jews had to accept the fact that wisdom is to be found among the Gentiles: this belief had long been recognized by the greatest rabbis in the past but had been abandoned in Eastern Europe as the result of persecution driving the Jews to intellectual isolation.

What was needed was first and foremost a pedagogic revolution: the Jews had to teach their children modern languages (especially German and Russian) and "secular" subjects such as arithmetic, geography, astronomy, and history, alongside modernized and more rational accounts of Jewish tradition. At the same time, a social and economic revolution was desperately required: the Jews had to abandon their age-old function as small-time traders, merchants, and moneylenders and become farmers, artisans, and members of the free professions. Moreover, as Jews they also had to purify and modernize the Hebrew language by making it into a medium for secular literary genres such as poetry, novels, plays, essays, newspapers, and modern "scientific" scholarship. All of these ideas had been part of the agenda of the early Enlightenment movement in Mendelssohn's days, but the linguistic plank had gradually been abandoned in favor of a turn to the German language alone as the medium of Jewish enlightenment. In the Russian Empire, where the Jews were conceived both by the government and by themselves as a unique "ethnic" group, there seemed to be no contradiction between the Jews using both Hebrew and Russian (or Polish in the semiautonomous "Kingdom of Poland") to transform themselves into "modern men" and thus ultimately to merit emancipation and equal rights.

For a small group of adherents of the Haskalah, however, already in the early 1870s the twin goals of emancipation and religious reform appeared not only as chimeras but as misguided dreams: the true solution to the plight of the Jews was to reawaken their "national consciousness," to reconceive them as a "nation" according to the new nationalist conceptions of nationhood.

The first thinker to articulate this new ideology was Peretz Smolenskin, who was born near the Belarusian city of Mogilev, moved first to Odessa—along with Vilnius an unofficial capital of the Russian Haskalah—and then, after traveling throughout Central and East Central Europe, settled in Vienna, the hotbed of nationalist sentiment among the many ethnic groups which comprised the Habsburg Empire. Smolenskin first distinguished himself by writing Hebrew novels in the spirit of the Haskalah, but for our purposes his most important venture was the founding of the periodical *Ha-Shahar* (The dawn) in 1868. At first, this journal was a rather standard advocate of Enlightenment ideology, but that began to change in 1872, when Smolenskin started to publish a series of long essays entitled "The Eternal People," "A Time for Action," and "A Time to Plant." Although these essays were long, meandering, and repetitive, Smolenskin's basic argument began from a strident anti-Mendelssohnian premise: the Jews were not a religion but a nation, from which logically followed an attack on the very concept of political emancipation as the guidepost to, and the goal of, the future of the Jews. These views he decried as not only wrong and harmful but ultimately self-destructive: they would inevitably lead to the "assimilation" of the Jews into the nations in which they lived, a process he believed was already happening in Western Europe. In these essays Smolenskin began a history-changing process: the creation of modern Jewish nationalism.

In this emerging worldview he was soon joined by a small group of readers, colleagues, and followers, the most important of whom were the Russian Jews Moshe Leib Lilienblum and Eliezer Perlman, who later changed his name to Eliezer Ben-Yehuda. Both had been born in traditional Jewish homes in Belarus, had lost their faith in traditional Judaism, and became adherents of the Haskalah movement, but soon took up Smolenskin's call for the revival of the Jews as a modern nation in their own right, on the model of the new nationalist movements in Europe. Indeed, Perlman/Ben-Yehuda went farther than his colleagues by insisting that Hebrew become the spoken "national language" of the Jewish people, and that this should happen nowhere else but in Palestine, their ancient home, which had to be revived as their modern national homeland. To this end, in 1878 he moved to Paris to study medicine, so as to be a "productive" member of a nascent

Hebrew-speaking nation in the Holy Land, and arrived in Jaffa in October 1881, where he and his wife began to raise the first family speaking modern Hebrew.

It was at this point that politics intruded in the form of the pogroms in the Russian Empire beginning in the spring of 1881. But before we turn to these events and their influence on the spread of modern Jewish nationalism and then of Zionism, we must step backward a bit and describe the efforts of several groups and individuals who were inspired by distinctly non-nationalist goals to improve the lot of the Jews already living in Palestine.

The most important such organization was the Alliance Israélite Universelle, founded in Paris in 1860 to improve the political, social, and economic conditions of the Jews around the world, but especially in North Africa and the Middle East, by teaching them how to become more "civilized" and thus merit emancipation. This primarily meant inculcating in them the values of modern "civilization" in the French mode and through the French language, but also making them more economically productive, primarily through training them in agriculture and artisan crafts. For this reason, in 1870 the Alliance founded Mikveh Yisrael, an agricultural school south of Jaffa, on land granted to them by the Turkish sultan. The goal of this school was to train Jews already in Palestine to found small agricultural settlements to sustain themselves economically. Tellingly, the leaders of the Alliance both in Paris and at Mikveh Yisrael actively opposed the burgeoning Jewish nationalist movement, as well as the very idea that foreign Jews should emigrate to Palestine. After the outbreak of the pogroms in 1881–82, they actively supported the emigration of Jews to the United States instead of the Holy Land.

But by then, history—to speak in rather grandiose terms—had changed in a radical fashion. Although the emigration of Jews from the Russian Empire had also begun before the outbreak of the pogroms and in response to the economic crisis both of the Empire itself and more specifically of the Jewish community, the violence against the Jews (which almost everyone believed—incorrectly, as we now know—was supported by the tsarist regime) helped to encourage masses of Jews to emigrate from Eastern Europe, to Western Europe and especially to the United States. A small minority of the emigrants, however, moved to Palestine in what was subsequently called in Zionist chronology the "First Aliyah" (the latter word literally meaning "ascent," as in the geographic and spiritual going up from the coastal plain of Palestine to Jerusalem in the hills of Judah). A good number of these emigrants did so for reasons very similar to those of their relatives and neighbors who emigrated to America or to South Africa: not as a result of political or religious ideology, but simply to seek a better life for themselves and their children.

But a small number of these immigrants did move to Palestine out of a firm, coherent, ideological motive: a belief in the ideas of modern Jewish nationalism, often inflected with utopian socialist or Tolstoyan views increasingly prevalent in the Russian Empire, especially among the young.

The most famous of these groups was founded in January 1882 by a group of university students in the city of Kharkov in Ukraine. Their society, known by its acronym Bilu (from Isaiah 2:5, "House of Jacob, come and let us go"), combined both nationalist and socialist ideals. At first, even the members of Bilu were uncertain about where they should move to in order to achieve their goals. Soon they agreed that the only suitable destination was Palestine, where they would create model egalitarian agricultural communities. About five hundred young Jews joined this movement, but most of them were unable or unwilling actually to move to the Holy Land to become farmers, and the first "Biluim" to arrive in Palestine consisted of a group of only fourteen people, which grew to fifty-three in the next few years. Faced with the challenges of agriculture in Palestine, many of these young idealists soon gave up and left Palestine, mostly for America.

Those who remained received training and aid from Mikveh Yisrael (despite the differences in their ideologies) and began to found small agricultural settlements.

In this effort they expected to receive far greater support from a much larger movement that emerged in the Russian Empire and in Romania in the early 1880s, known as Love of Zion. One of the most important ideologues of this movement was the physician Leon Pinsker, who was at first a supporter of the Haskalah but was dissuaded from its goals by the outbreak of the pogroms. On January 1, 1882, he published a pamphlet in German entitled *Autoemancipation* that argued that anti-Jewish sentiments were so entrenched in European society that they could not be overcome by the emancipation of the Jews, however much the latter strove to "improve" themselves along the lines of Enlightenment ideology. Accepting the new nationalist definition of the Jews, he believed that the only solution for the Jews was to leave Europe and found a self-sustaining national territory. Although he was at first not certain where that territory ought to be (perhaps in Argentina or other countries with large stretches of unsettled lands), he soon came around to the view that that national territory could only be Palestine, given its historical significance and the emotional attachment of the Jewish masses to it, and he quickly became a major and highly influential leader of the nascent Love of Zion movement.

One of the tasks of that movement was indeed to support the emigration of Jews to Palestine to establish self-supporting agricultural communities there, but the Love of Zion movement was far less ideologically uniform than Bilu, always strapped for funds, and hampered by legal restrictions imposed by the Russian government. Thus, it could not solve the serious problems of the small number of Jewish agricultural settlements actually established in Palestine, which soon appealed for help to the French Jewish philanthropist Baron Edmond de Rothschild. Baron Edmond acceded to this request, and his financial support was indeed crucial to the survival of these new settlements, though even with his help, many failed due to the inexperience of their members and the harsh terrain and health hazards of Palestine.

Moreover, Rothschild's motivation was entirely philanthropic and stridently opposed to the ideological aims not only of modern Jewish nationalism but especially (and quite naturally—he was, after all, a Rothschild) to the socialist ideals of many of the settlers. Indeed, the growing number of settlements that abandoned Jewish religious law significantly diminished his enthusiasm for this enterprise. Perhaps even more shocking to his sensibilities was the decision, in 1887, of the small number of religious Jews among the settlers, following the dictates of the majority of Orthodox rabbis both in Palestine and in Eastern Europe, that the agricultural settlements he subsidized cease their harvest of crops that year, since it was a sabbatical year in which Biblical law forbade Jews in the Land of Israel from cultivating their agricultural fields or consuming its produce. Although attempts were made by some Orthodox rabbis to solve the problem by engaging in the legal fiction of selling the land to non-Jews, the baron found this solution as appalling as the heterodox socialism of the secular, and even anti-religious, settlers. As a result, he lost interest in the project, shifting his support to aiding the millions of Jews who were emigrating from Eastern Europe to the New World.

Moreover, the Love of Zion movement itself lost much of its appeal as the violence against the Jews began to dissipate in the mid-1880s and ceased in the 1890s, and perhaps even more importantly as it was beset by formidable ideological rifts within its ranks. Most influential was the Hebrew writer Asher Ginsberg, who wrote under the pseudonym Ahad Ha'am ("one of the people"). Although this name implied a populist perspective, he was as far from populism as possible: a self-conscious intellectual elitist, he argued forcefully that the entire enterprise of supporting mass Jewish emigration to Palestine and, even more important, that the political goal of attaining a sovereign Jewish homeland was an ideological and practical error, since it misunderstood the basic goal of modern Jewish nationalism, which was to forge a national cultural renaissance among the Jews, primarily through the revival of the Hebrew language and culture. To this Ahad Ha'am added his own complex views regarding the transmutation of the teachings of traditional Judaism into modern, and distinctly secular, philosophical concepts, influenced by a motley group of European thinkers including positivists, Social Darwinists, and Nietzsche. Only after training an elite avant-garde of those who espoused his philosophy would any emigration to Palestine, or political activity in support of political sovereignty, be appropriate. Soon, his version of modern Jewish nationalism was dubbed "spiritual" or "cultural Zionism," as opposed to "political Zionism." To understand these terms, we must move beyond the invention of modern Jewish nationalism and its early embodiment in movements such as the Bilu and Lovers of Zion to the creation of the Zionist movement itself.

Chapter 3
Theodor Herzl and the creation of the Zionist movement, 1897–1917

The actual term "Zionism"—or, more precisely, the German *Zionismus*—was invented in 1890 by the Jewish nationalist Nathan Birnbaum in his journal *Selbstemanzipation*. But the term attained by far its most important and long-lived importance through the work and writings of the man universally credited with the founding of the Zionist movement, Theodor Herzl.

Herzl was an extraordinarily complex figure, much of whose inner life still remains mysterious even after the scores of biographies and studies written about him. He was born in Budapest in 1860 into a typical upper-middle-class Jewish family, whose language and culture was German and whose basic aspirations were for social and economic mobility. Although many have claimed that he had absolutely no connection with Judaism before his turn to Zionism, that is not factually correct: he and his family worshipped at a liberal temple and, more importantly, never repudiated his legal inclusion in the Jewish community—something that was possible in the Austro-Hungarian and German Empires, and to some extent popular among Jews of backgrounds such as his.

More precisely, like tens of thousands of Jewish intellectuals throughout Europe in his time and place (and largely of his upper-middle-class status), he believed, in the first decades of his life, that his Jewishness was entirely an accident of birth that had no serious bearing on his life, thought, or his future; even his encounter with anti-Semitism at university did not dissuade him from this fundamental conviction. Although trained as a lawyer at the University of Vienna, his true aspiration was to be a playwright, a goal he pursued, with minor success, until his death. Meanwhile, he made his living as an essayist and a journalist, and from October 1891 to July 1895 was posted to Paris as a foreign correspondent of one of the most important liberal newspapers of his day, and certainly of the German-speaking lands, the Viennese *Neue Freie Presse*. In 1895 he returned to Vienna and served as the cultural editor of the paper, thus wielding substantial cultural power in the Austrian capital and throughout the German-speaking world, but having nothing to do with his views on the "Jewish problem."

During his stay in Paris, he witnessed—and covered for his newspaper—the beginnings of the "Dreyfus affair," which began in 1894 with the conviction on a charge of espionage of Captain Alfred Dreyfus, a Jewish officer in the French army. The controversy about Dreyfus's innocence or guilt turned into the most important political crisis in French politics at the end of the nineteenth and beginning of the twentieth centuries, until its resolution with the complete exoneration of Dreyfus in 1906. Until recently it was universally believed that Herzl's witnessing of the anti-Semitism unleashed by the Dreyfus affair converted him into a Zionist. After close examination of his writings on the affair by several historians, this has proven to be utterly untrue: like most Jews in France, after Dreyfus's initial arrest Herzl was worried that the captain was actually guilty of the charge against him, though obviously hopeful that he was not. It was only after he became a Zionist and began to view the world through Zionist lenses that Herzl came—not surprisingly—to apply a Zionist diagnosis to the Dreyfus affair.

But the matter is far more complicated than that: not only do many authors and books still repeat the claim of the crucial effect of the affair on Herzl becoming a Zionist, Herzl himself adopted this myth in his own retrospective writings and "self-fashionings."

What is clear is that sometime in the mid-1890s Herzl did become convinced that anti-Semitism was a permanent and inexorable feature of European society which would not disappear, in line with the Enlightenment belief that as progress spread throughout the world, all such prejudices would necessarily disappear. Although by no means abandoning his belief in the basic idea of progress and the superiority of European over other civilizations, he came gradually to believe that the Jews constituted a nation rather than a religious community, and that the only solution to anti-Semitism was that the Jews leave Europe and found their own national homeland elsewhere. Like Pinsker, he was at first not at all convinced that this homeland had to be in Palestine—Argentina was another possibility. But soon he came around to that conclusion that the Jewish masses of Eastern Europe would support such an idea only if it was in the Land of Israel.

The fascinating historical conundrum is that Herzl came to these views entirely without knowledge of the writings of the modern Jewish nationalists, of the Bilu or the Love of Zion movements, of the controversies between the supporters of Ahad Ha'am and their opponents within the nationalist camp. Indeed, he could not even have read most of their writings, as he did not know Hebrew. But even those works that were published in German were unknown to Herzl until after he became a Zionist. This was a rare case of independent ideological gestation.

His first attempt to put his ideas into practice was to convince major Jewish philanthropists to support his ideas. But he failed to convince them of his solution to the Jewish problem, which they deemed completely impractical and ideologically dangerous, especially since the admission that the Jews could not be integrated into European societies could put at risk Jewish communities which were fighting for their basic rights against the anti-Semites in their midst.

While still appealing for financial support from the Jewish plutocracy, Herzl put his ideas into writing, most importantly in his book *Der Judenstaat*, written in 1895 and published a year later. The title of this small book is usually translated into English as *The Jewish State*, whereas the far more precise rendering is "The Jews' state." This is not a pedantic quibble, but a matter that goes to the very heart of Herzl's worldview: the "state" that he imagined was *for* the Jews rather than being defined as "Jewish" by Judaic culture of any sort, traditional or modernist, including the modern Hebrew nationalism of thinkers such as Ahad Ha'am, who therefore viewed Herzl quite simply as an ignorant interloper into matters of which he had no knowledge.

Herzl's Zionism was thus purely political both in theory and in practice: the Jews as a nation did not need a new culture or a new language or a new concept of the messianic era, but only one thing: a national polity of their own, whose creation would solve forever the problem of anti-Semitism both for the Jews themselves and for Europe as a whole. Once all Jews who desired to remain Jews emigrated to their own land, those who did not want to do so would disappear into the nations and nation-states in which they lived. This process had no cultural corollary, no necessary transformation of the Jews as Jews: in their own state they could speak whatever language they chose, practice Judaism (or not) in any form, and continue to engage in cosmopolitan bourgeois European culture.

Indeed, there was a distinct liberal utopian streak in Herzl's vision of the Jews' state: most famously, in *Der Judenstaat* he called for the institution of a seven-hour workday, and his design for the flag of this state was comprised of seven five-pointed yellow stars (not the six-pointed Stars of David) against a white backdrop, to symbolize this economic and social progressivism. More fundamentally, his basic notion of a state did not conform to the standard contemporary definition of a polity with a fixed legislature, executive, and judiciary; it would instead be a federation of self-governing communities banding together voluntarily for the minimum of functions necessary for survival. This state would have no clerical hierarchy, no state religion, and no standing army, since it would have no need for one.

This raises one of the most controversial issues that have dominated debates over Zionism from Herzl's day to the present. It is frequently alleged that the Zionists took no notice of the fact that the vast majority of the population of Palestine were Arabs, and that this reality would immensely complicate the plan for a Jewish homeland in Palestine. This is, however, incorrect: the "Arab problem" had been raised by Zionists such as Ahad Ha'am long before Herzl, and then by Herzl himself in a clear and frontal manner, though one unacceptable to later supporters of Palestinian nationalism: he believed that the transformation of Palestine into a progressive modern state, with an economic system based on the most up-to-date scientific principles of agriculture and industry, would inevitably improve the lot of the Arab population of Palestine immensely, relieving them of the yoke of feudalism under which they lived and of the unfair Ottoman rule which exploited them both economically and politically. They would therefore inevitably come to see Zionism as beneficial to them as well as to the Jews.

This view was regarded as utterly naïve not only by the anti- and non-Zionists who regarded the demographic reality of Palestine as a—if not *the*—major obstacle to the Zionist project but also by many others within the Zionist ranks, who struggled with this problem for the decades to come.

The other major obstacle to the implementation of the Zionist plan was the simple fact that Palestine was controlled by the Ottoman Empire, and there was no reason to assume that the

Ottomans would even consider granting this part of their holdings to the Jews. To this Herzl had yet another simple (if to others utterly unrealistic) solution: since the Ottoman Empire was suffering from an acute economic crisis, which was already leading to loss of power and prestige not only within its borders but also—or especially—around the world, these problems could be solved by a massive infusion of capital into the Ottoman coffers by Jewish bankers from abroad. Again, the fact that these bankers had absolutely no interest in participating in such a scheme and indeed regarded it as ludicrous did not sway Herzl from believing that it was the most rational solution to the problem at hand.

And if the Ottomans could not be persuaded to give up Palestine voluntarily, Herzl reasoned, they could be pressured into doing so by the other great powers of Europe. He then embarked on what became the political goal of the rest of his short life: securing from these powers active support for the Zionist project, through what came to be called a "charter"—a diplomatic instrument granting the Jews the right to a homeland in Palestine. To this end he used every means at his disposal to secure support of the great powers. At first, the German kaiser expressed some interest in the plan—not out of concern for the Jews but to gain a strategic foothold in the Middle East—and even granted Herzl two personal audiences to put forward his ideas. But soon the kaiser lost interest, and Herzl turned his attention to Germany's rivals, who were as unsupportive of the plan as the German emperor.

However, although Herzl received almost no support from the two constituencies he most avidly courted—the wealthy Jews and the great powers of Europe—he was received with enormous enthusiasm, and often true adulation, by masses of Jews in Eastern Europe and the Balkans. Wherever he traveled in these lands, Jews crowded in the streets by the thousands, hailing him as the "King of the Jews"—even though their rabbinic leaders denounced Herzl as a heretical scoundrel out to destroy Judaism by disobeying God's commandments. The reasons for Herzl's personal popularity

1. Theodor Herzl created the Zionist movement in the late nineteenth century and summoned its first congress in 1897 in Basel, Switzerland. This photograph by the Zionist artist Ephraim Lilien became a canonical image of Herzl, looking over the Rhine but pondering Zion in his mind.

have been dissected at length in the scholarly and popular literature, but were undoubtedly the result of three factors. First, he looked the part: an aristocratic bearing with a black beard and piercing eyes that have often been described as resembling that of an ancient Assyrian king—an "exotic" look deemed "Semitic" but not regarded as typical Jewish looks. Indeed, the very fact that he was a famous figure in the non-Jewish world gave him a stature which was admired by many Jews—a variation of the well-known, if still not entirely understood, phenomenon of the power of the outsider coming from the periphery of a society as opposed to an insider from its center, something most commonly associated with figures such as Napoleon or Stalin. Perhaps even less susceptible to rational historical explanation is that Herzl exuded what his contemporary the German sociologist Max Weber defined as "charisma": the quality of an extraordinary personality, by virtue of which he (or she) is believed to be set apart from ordinary people and viewed as endowed with exceptional qualities either of divine origin or exemplary of someone destined to be a leader and to be treated as such.

Whatever the explanation, Herzl played his part with consummate skill, and succeeded in doing what none of his predecessors had not: convening an international conference of supporters of Zionism, which he dubbed the "Zionist Congress." Herzl had planned to hold this congress in Munich, but the united opposition of the rabbis of that city—both liberal and Orthodox—forced him to move the venue of the meeting to Basel, where it met from August 29 to August 31, 1897. Inevitably, there were already fundamental disagreements within the various constituencies in this newly founded movement, but Herzl dominated the proceedings, along with Max Nordau, an even more internationally renowned German writer and controversial public figure whom he designated as his chief lieutenant. Ultimately, the various factions agreed to what was called the "Basel program":

> Zionism seeks to establish a home for the Jewish people in Palestine secured under public law. The Congress contemplates the following means to the attainment of this end: 1) The promotion by appropriate means of the settlement in Palestine of Jewish farmers, artisans, and manufacturers; 2) the organization and uniting of the whole of Jewry by means of appropriate institutions, both local and

international in accordance with the laws of each country; 3) the
strengthening and fostering of Jewish national sentiment and
national consciousness; and 4) preparatory steps toward obtaining
the consent of governments, where necessary, in order to reach the
goal of Zionism.

Each plank of this program and its careful wording was negotiated
and debated within the many subcommittees of the congress;
particular attention ought to be paid to four phrases. First, there is
no mention here of the word "state," not to speak of a "Jewish state";
this term was rejected by some delegates (particularly by followers
of "spiritual Zionism") on ideological grounds; others worried that
it would be politically incendiary, particularly to the Ottoman
Empire. Similarly, there is no mention of a "homeland" (not to
speak of a "Jewish homeland"): the English "home" is an imprecise
rendering of the German *Heimstätte*, which more technically
ought to be defined as a "homestead"—a term which usually
connotes a dwelling place rather than a political entity but whose
very vagueness made it acceptable to the majority of the delegates.
Thirdly, the term "public law" referred to no known body of law
such as the later "international law." And finally, "in accordance
with the laws of each country" was a carefully worked-out formula
meant to assuage those who were worried about the effect of the
program on the safety of Jews in lands in which they were being
actively persecuted and were struggling for basic, not to speak of
equal, rights. Crucial, too, is the absence in the Basel program of
any mention of the renaissance of Jewish culture or the Hebrew
language, as opposed to "the strengthening and fostering of Jewish
national sentiment and national consciousness": the former would
be objectionable not only to Herzl, Nordau, and the other strictly
"political Zionists" but also to the very small minority of delegates
who were traditional Jews or rabbis who rejected any connection
between Zionism and any secular, cultural, renaissance.

Notwithstanding all these compromises, the First Zionist
Congress was a great success for Herzl: he became the president of

2. The Second Zionist Congress was held in Basel in August 1898. Herzl insisted that all delegates wear formal attire—much to the chagrin of the Russian delegates.

a movement that he had been struggling to create since the idea of Zionism entered into his mind, an idea that had faced so much opposition. After the end of the First Zionist Congress he wrote in his diary: "Were I to sum up the Basel Congress in a word—which I shall guard against pronouncing publicly—it would be this: 'At Basel, I founded the Jewish State.' If I said this out loud today, I would be answered by universal laughter. If not in five years, certainly in fifty, everyone will know it." Herzl's followers have often pointed out that precisely fifty years and seventy-seven days later, on November 29, 1947, the General Assembly of the United Nations voted to partition Palestine into independent Jewish and Arab states, and just over fifty and a half years after he wrote those words, the independent State of Israel was created on May 14, 1948.

These events were highly contingent on totally unforeseeable political realities in the post–World War II era. But more relevant

here is the fact that Herzl's success at the First Zionist Congress
did not resolve the fundamental ideological divides within the
Zionist movement. Thus, there were at least three organized
groupings within the Zionist movement that differed from Herzl's
strictly "political" Zionism: First, Ahad Ha'am and his followers
soon organized themselves as the "Democratic Faction," which
insisted on a cultural revolution within the Jewish community
based on secular Hebrew culture, but also distrusted Herzl
personally and opposed what they considered his near-dictatorial
control of the movement. Secondly, already in 1899, the first
socialist Zionist group was founded, which soon divided into
many different groups and subgroups, often based on crucial
differences such as acceptance of Marxian or so-called "utopian"
socialism, support of Yiddish as well as Hebrew as the national
language(s) of the Jewish people, and on solutions to the "Arab
problem" in Palestine, and also—like so many other movements
on the left—on far subtler disagreements in the theory of
socialism. And finally, in 1902 the Mizrachi movement was
founded to put forward a synthesis between Orthodox Judaism
and Zionism.

Ironically, the Orthodox Zionists came to side with Herzl on some
crucial issues facing the Zionist movement as a whole, since they
considered far more dangerous—and, quite literally, heretical—the
cultural and social programs of the "spiritual" and socialist
Zionists. This was nowhere more evident than in the huge fracas
that emerged within the Zionist movement at its Sixth Congress,
held in Basel from August 23 to August 28, 1903, at which Herzl
presented to the movement a proposal he had recently received
from the British government: that an autonomous Jewish
colony be established in Uganda in British East Africa (not
geographically coterminous with the current state of Uganda).
Herzl regarded this offer with great enthusiasm as a great
diplomatic coup: one of the great powers was, in his view, in this
way endorsing the very idea of a *Judenstaat*. He repeatedly
insisted to the Congress that this proposal did not in the least

depart from the Basel Program and its profound support (and his own) for Palestine as the only homeland of the Jewish people; the Uganda colony would merely serve as a temporary haven for persecuted Jews, especially those in the Russian Empire—who were recently the victims of the most severe pogrom to occur since the early 1880s, the Kishinev pogrom that had broken out on April 6–7, 1903. In an oft-cited phrase, Nordau described the Uganda proposal as merely a *Nachtasyl*—a night asylum—for Jews needing to escape their oppressors.

But the vast majority of the Eastern European delegates to the Sixth Congress (joined by others from different parts of the world, including America) viewed what they called the "Uganda scheme" as proof positive of Herzl and Nordau's utter disengagement from any authentic Jewish concerns; to them, the Land of Israel was the only possible venue for the historical and spiritual homeland of the Jewish people, and accepting the Uganda idea even as a temporary measure would constitute a slippery slope to the suicide of the Zionist dream. Moreover, only a few months before advancing the Uganda proposal, Herzl had traveled to Saint Petersburg and met there with the notoriously anti-Semitic Russian minister of the interior, Vyacheslav von Plehve, a personification, for the Russian Zionists, of the hated tsarist regime which (they thought) had recently perpetrated the Kishinev massacre. In his mind, Herzl was merely participating in hard-nosed realpolitik: even if the Russian government wanted to support the Zionist movement out of a desire to rid itself of Jews it hated, that support could still be useful to the Zionists, especially given the historic rivalry between the Russian and Turkish Empires in the Near East in general, and over the "holy sites" in Palestine in particular.

But for the Russian Zionists, Herzl's realpolitik was merely a synonym for collaboration with the devil, not for the benefit of the Jewish people but for his own glorification, and thus, when the Uganda proposal came to the floor of the Sixth Zionist Congress, they staged a massive walkout from the Congress, and because of this split the fate of the movement seemed to be hanging in the balance. After furious negotiations they agreed to return to the Congress and let the matter be put to a vote. Crucially (a point that is often misrepresented), the Mizrachi delegates—who as Orthodox Jews prayed daily for the return of the Jews to the Holy Land and thus might be assumed to have led the charge against the Uganda plan—actually voted *for* it; again, this was a demonstration of both their loyalty to Herzl and their opposition to, and fear of, the Ahad Ha'amists, socialists, and other secular Zionists. In the end, Herzl did manage to muster a majority vote of 295–178, not precisely to endorse the proposal but to send an "investigatory commission" to East Africa to examine the proposed territory and report its findings for the next congress.

Despite this technical victory, the Uganda affair not only seriously diminished Herzl's standing within the Zionist movement as a whole; it undoubtedly played a major factor in his declining health, and less than a year later, on July 3, 1904, he died in Vienna, at the age of forty-four. Even his most bitter enemies within the Zionist movement mourned this terrible end to an extraordinary life: in Basel Theodor Herzl may not have "created the Jewish State," but unlike anyone before him, he created a credible Zionist movement out of what others had dismissed as a naïve dream. The Jewish world would never be the same again.

Chapter 4

The Weizmann era and the Balfour Declaration

Herzl's death did not mean an end to the Zionist movement, but even his most talented and trusted colleagues could not replace him in an effective manner. The next presidents of the World Zionist Organization were competent but uninspiring leaders of a movement that lost its momentum in the decade after Herzl's death. But somewhat ironically (given the centrality of Europe in the Zionist movement), the most notable and long-lived accomplishments of Zionism in these years occurred in Palestine itself and outside the purview of the official Zionist mainstream.

First and foremost, the decade between 1904 and 1914 witnessed the "Second Aliyah," the emigration to Palestine of roughly forty thousand Jews, mainly from the Russian Empire. As in the First Aliyah, once more a large number of these immigrants were not motivated by radical political and religious views, but the most vocal and influential among them were imbued with far more thoroughgoing socialist ideas than their predecessors. By far the most important and long-lasting creation of the Second Aliyah was the collective settlement, at first called the *kevuzah* and then kibbutz: a communistic egalitarian agricultural community in which all private property was forbidden, the "means of production" were held in common, jobs were assigned by rotation, and there was to be absolute equality between the sexes. So far-reaching was this collectivism that even the most basic unit of society, the nuclear family, was subject to its radical ideology. All children were separated from their parents, reared together in a "children's home," and permitted to visit with their parents for only a short time each afternoon, during the latter's rest period. This put into practice Marx's call in the *Communist Manifesto* for the abolition of the "bourgeois family," and was ultimately the most extensive collectivization of childrearing in the twentieth century, unmatched by the later collective farms of the Soviet Union or China. The theory was that this form of childrearing would create psychologically healthy and independent children and undo the psychic damage caused by what Freud was beginning to analyze as the pathologies of the parent-child dynamic.

The first kibbutz was founded south of the Sea of Galilee in 1909 and named Degania, Hebrew for cornflower, and in the next decade eleven more collective settlements were created. But the influence of the kibbutzim went far beyond their small numbers. They were revered as the purest expression of both Zionism and socialism, and in due course the source of many of the most important political, cultural, and military leaders of the bourgeoning Jewish community in Palestine. From the start, however, the kibbutzim were split by profound ideological rifts so common in left-wing politics—from communist Marxists, to "utopian socialists," to proponents of the thought of Aaron David Gordon, a Russian Jew who immigrated to Palestine in 1904 and propounded an ideology based more on Tolstoy than on Marx in its adulation of the life of the farmer and the purity of manual labor. Calling on the Jewish people to reject what he viewed as their profoundly unhealthy alienation from nature, Gordon charged them with the twin goals of the "conquest of labor" and the "conquest of the land" and as such was one of the most influential thinkers of Labor Zionism in Palestine.

One of the sharpest disagreements between the settlers of the First and Second Aliyot and indeed among the divergent subgroups of the latter was the thorny question of the role of Arab labor in the new Zionist settlements. The older communities had relied on Arab farmers both as manual laborers and for their deep knowledge of the land of Palestine and methods of farming its problematic soil. But to the most left-wing groups that formed collective settlements in the period 1904–1914, the hiring of Arab workers was rejected, since it worked against the creation of a self-sustaining Jewish agricultural class and because it smacked of "bourgeois oppression" of the working class. Ironically, the bearers of this ideology in time became the most forceful advocates of what would be called a "binational" form of Zionism, calling for a joint Jewish-Arab commonwealth in Palestine.

Meanwhile, however, the new settlements had to confront the issue of Arab violence against their communities, and they created the first self-defense units of Jewish Palestine. How to reconcile this armed struggle with the goal of Jewish-Arab coexistence became a major ideological challenge to the several socialist Zionist groupings in Palestine (and by extension in the Diaspora as well).

At the same time, a very different form of Jewish life in Palestine was being created: the city of Tel Aviv, founded on the outskirts of the ancient town of Jaffa in 1909. To be sure, Jews had lived in the major cities of Palestine—Jaffa, Jerusalem, Haifa, Hebron, Safed—since antiquity, and their numbers had grown in the years since the First Aliyah. But the creation of Tel Aviv betokened something entirely new: a Hebrew-speaking modern Jewish city that departed from the life of the Orthodox (or those now called "Ultra-Orthodox") Jewish dwellers in the so-called holy cities of Palestine who subsisted largely on charity from Jews in the Diaspora. Although its population grew only to roughly 1,500 inhabitants by 1914, Tel Aviv provided a crucial counterpoint to the kibbutz and later, less collectivist agricultural settlements such as the *moshav*—a farming village made up of privately-owned plots and homes sharing agricultural implements as well as an equal distribution of profits. The new urban Jewish population provided a new commercial paradigm for the realization of the Zionist dream.

That dream was to be shaken to its core by the outbreak of the World War in 1914. The Ottoman authorities arrested and exiled many of the leaders of the Zionist movement in Palestine, who, as Russian subjects, were now considered enemy aliens. More broadly, the war put the future of the Ottoman Empire as a whole into doubt: If the Ottomans were defeated, who would control their territories, including Palestine? From virtually the start of the hostilities Britain set its eyes on conquering the entire Middle East and began intensive, if often secret, negotiations with various Arab leaders to achieve this goal. Thus, in a letter written in October 1915 by Sir Henry McMahon, the British high commissioner in Egypt, to Sharif Hussein bin Ali, the emir of Mecca who led the "Arab Revolt" against the Ottomans, the British government declared its support for Arab independence and control by the Hashemite dynasty over vast stretches of territory, including "the districts of Mersina and Alexandretta, and portions of Syria lying to the west of the districts of Damascus, Homs, Hama, and Aleppo." Whether this promise included the territory of Palestine soon became a matter of grave contention, central to the future of the country.

Indeed, from the start of the war Zionists in countries on both sides of the battlegrounds faced a dilemma entirely analogous to that of the socialist parties of Europe: the latter were in theory committed to an internationalism that opposed nationalism as a force used by the bourgeoisie to waylay the proletariat from its class solidarity. However, as war fever mounted in each country, the pull of patriotism all but overwhelmed the national parties' commitment to the international working class: the majorities of the French, German, Russian, and many smaller Socialist parties voted to support the war, arguing in each case that the victory of its side would immeasurably aid the socialist cause around the world.

Exactly the same scenario occurred within the Zionist movements of the warring nations: the majority of the Russian, British, and French Zionists believed that their cause would be enormously advanced by the defeat of Germany, Austria, and especially the Ottoman Empire; the majority of German, Austrian, and Ottoman Zionists believed that their cause would be accomplished with the defeat not only of the British and French but especially of the evil tsarist regime, the mortal enemy of the Jewish people.

In this inter-Zionist debate, by far the most consequential figure—and soon to be only second in importance to Herzl in Zionist history—was Chaim Weizmann. Born in 1874 to a middle-class Jewish family in the small town of Motol, Belarus, Weizmann attended gymnasium in the nearby city of Pinsk, and then moved to Darmstadt, Germany, where he studied chemistry, followed by stints at the Technische Hochschule of Berlin and then at the University of Fribourg in Switzerland, from which he received his doctorate in chemistry in 1899. Soon thereafter he accepted a position as lecturer in organic chemistry at the University of Geneva, where he taught until 1904, when he moved—fatefully—to Manchester University. While still in Russia he had abandoned the traditional Jewish faith in which he was raised to become a convinced Zionist and follower of Ahad Ha'am. Indeed, at several Zionist Congresses he forcefully led the Democratic Faction in opposition to Herzl's policies; his maiden speech at the Zionist Congress of 1901 was in support of the establishment of a Hebrew university in Palestine, a keystone of Ahad Ha'am's platform.

In the years after Herzl's death, however, Weizmann gradually moved to a position combining cultural and political Zionism, and he soon emerged as one of the leading figures in the influential Manchester Zionist movement and then, in 1917, became president of the British Zionist Federation. By this time he was quite renowned as a chemist, and several of his inventions played a role in the British war effort. (Indeed, a bacterium crucial to the manufacturing of several explosives and new types of fuel and synthetic rubber is called the "Weizmann organism" in honor of its inventor.) In this capacity Weizmann had access to the most important political figures in Britain, including Arthur Balfour, the former prime minister who was serving as secretary of state for foreign affairs in the cabinet of Lloyd George. Weizmann achieved some success with Balfour on the basis of the latter's Protestant convictions regarding the ties of the Jews to the Holy Land.

But far more important was Weizmann's ability, in the summer and fall of 1917, to convince Balfour, and through him the British cabinet, that the Jews in both Russia and the United States were absolutely crucial to their respective countries' remaining in the world war. In the former, the Provisional Government had come to power in the wake of Tsar Nicholas II's abdication in February and was now frayed to the point of near extinction, with the most prominent supporters of the war effort being forced to resign and the Bolsheviks and their antiwar policy gaining strength in Saint Petersburg and Moscow. At the same time, the United States had declared war on Germany in April 1917 and had sent a modest, if significant, number of troops to the front, but there was still massive opposition in the country to the embroilment of Americans in a European war, and President Wilson was not able to convince Congress to declare war on Austria-Hungary in addition to Germany.

Against this backdrop, Weizmann was able to convince His Majesty's Government that if the British were to support the Zionist cause, it would be repaid handsomely by the Jews in both the United States and in Russia, who—so Weizmann argued persistently and ultimately persuasively—had so much political influence in their respective countries that they could sway public opinion and the seats of power to have the countries remain in the war.

In reality, this was at best smoke and mirrors on Weizmann's part: the Jews in the United States had virtually no political influence at this time, and certainly no ability to change the opinions of the opponents of the war in Congress or in the country at large. In Russia, the Jews had absolutely no influence on the Provisional Government, and while many of the leaders of the Bolshevik movement were indeed of Jewish origin, they uniformly regarded that background as entirely superseded by their communism, and in any event they all regarded Zionism as an evil reactionary tool of the Jewish bourgeoisie in its class warfare on the proletariat. But these facts were totally ignored (or misrepresented) by Weizmann, who succeeded in playing brilliantly on the stereotype of worldwide Jewish political power propounded at great length around the world in the infamous *Protocols of the Elders of Zion* or by individual anti-Semites like Henry Ford. To be sure, the timing of this lobbying effort was also crucial, as the British forces in the Middle East led by General Edmund Allenby had by late October 1917 advanced to the Gaza-Beersheba line and were a scant fifty miles away from conquering both Jerusalem and Jaffa, and thus were all but certain to control the fate of Palestine after the war.

And so, on November 2, 1917, Lord Balfour sent the following letter to Lionel Walter Rothschild, the president of the British Zionist Federation:

Dear Lord Rothschild,

I have much pleasure in conveying to you, on behalf of His Majesty's Government, the following declaration of sympathy with Jewish Zionist aspirations which has been submitted to, and approved by, the Cabinet.

"His Majesty's Government view with favour the establishment in Palestine of a national home for the Jewish people, and will use their best endeavours to facilitate the achievement of this object, it being clearly understood that nothing shall be done which may prejudice the civil and religious rights of existing non-Jewish communities in Palestine, or the rights and political status enjoyed by Jews in any other country."

DOCUMENT 1.
The Balfour Declaration.

Foreign Office,
November 2nd, 1917.

Dear Lord Rothschild,

I have much pleasure in conveying to you, on behalf of His Majesty's Government, the following declaration of sympathy with Jewish Zionist aspirations which has been submitted to, and approved by, the Cabinet.

"His Majesty's Government view with favour the establishment in Palestine of a national home for the Jewish people, and will use their best endeavours to facilitate the achievement of this object, it being clearly understood that nothing shall be done which may prejudice the civil and religious rights of existing non-Jewish communities in Palestine, or the rights and political status enjoyed by Jews in any other country"

I should be grateful if you would bring this declaration to the knowledge of the Zionist Federation.

[signature: Arthur James Balfour]

3. On November 2, 1917, British foreign secretary Arthur Balfour sent a letter to Lord Lionel Rothschild, a leading British Zionist, announcing that the British government "view[ed] with favour the establishment in Palestine of a national home for the Jewish people." This letter became known as the Balfour Declaration and was regarded as a tremendous victory for the Zionist movement.

I should be grateful if you would bring this declaration to the knowledge of the Zionist Federation.

Yours sincerely, Arthur James Balfour

Every word of this document had been carefully debated by the British government: first, this was definitely not a "charter for Palestine" of the sort campaigned for by Herzl. Britain did not grant Palestine to the Zionists; it could not have done so, since it did not (yet) control Palestine or have any authority to dispose of any of the territories of the Ottoman Empire, which was still very alive in early November 1917. What the British did give the Zionists was a promissory note: Britain "looked with sympathy on Zionist aspirations"; it "viewed with favor" the establishment of a Jewish national home in Palestine. Note, here, the crucial article: "a," not "the," Jewish national home, thus at least in theory keeping in play other Jewish national homes in other parts of the world. Most crucial were the next two clauses, which were later to become the subject of unending differing interpretations by the two sides: the Balfour Declaration committed Great Britain to "use its best efforts to facilitate the achievement of a Jewish national home in Palestine," but that was followed by "it being clearly understood that nothing shall be done which may prejudice the civil and religious rights of existing non-Jewish communities in Palestine, or the rights and political status enjoyed by Jews in any other country." Did the latter phrase serve as a condition for the first?

In due course, this debate would have life-and-death consequences for the Jews in Palestine and the success or failure of the Zionist enterprise. But in November 1917, the Zionist movement as a whole was utterly elated by the receipt of the Balfour Declaration: Weizmann had succeeded where Herzl had failed! A—if not *the*—major world power had promised Palestine to the Jews for a "national home." The Zionist goal first defined in the Basel Program was now within reach.

Chapter 5
Socialist and Revisionist Zionisms, 1917–1939

For the two decades following the Balfour Declaration, Chaim Weizmann remained the dominant leader of the Zionist movement worldwide. His intimate ties to the British government became even more central to the success of the movement as Britain gained control over Palestine in the "mandate system" created by the League of Nations after the debacle of the World War. Indeed, the very document that created the British Mandate over Palestine included the Balfour Declaration in its text, linking the fate of the Jewish homeland to Britain's control of the territory. In this way, Weizmann's great coup of 1917 was now recognized not just by the British authorities but also by the international community at large—and by the emerging entity called "international law."

Externally, two developments began to call into question Britain's commitment to Zionism: first, it became clear that the Balfour Declaration had quite clearly not said anything about the borders of Palestine; it merely promised that a Jewish home was to be "in" Palestine. And thus it came as a shock to a significant part of the Zionist movement when, in 1920, the British government began to give clear signals that it was seriously considering separating "Transjordan" from Palestine, a move necessitated by the promises the government had given to Arab leaders regarding control of this territory after the war. These were almost entirely parallel to the promises embedded in the Balfour Declaration, and had even more importance as Britain sought to placate the Hashemite ruling family. Thus, on March 21, 1921, the British government announced the establishment of the Kingdom of Transjordan as an independent state, severing the territories many Zionists regarded as Eastern and Western Palestine. In the coming years this act would be one of the causes for a major schism within the Zionist movement, and it served as the first of a long series of moves by the British authorities that struck the Zionist leadership as backtracking on the promises of the Balfour Declaration.

The second major external factor affecting the Zionist movement in these years was the gradual rise and consolidation of the Palestinian national movement, whose dynamics were in many ways parallel to those of the Zionist movement, if delayed by a decade or so. The spread of Palestinian nationalism invariably led to a sharp rise in Arab opposition to the Zionist enterprise on every front. This opposition took the form of increasingly violent attacks against the Jewish community in Palestine, economic actions on the ground such as a general strike, and massive lobbying with the British authorities to block any further Jewish immigration and indeed to rescind support for the very idea of a Jewish homeland in the Land of Israel.

But before entering into both of these minefields, we must turn our attention to a phenomenon that was certainly noted at the time but whose implications would become clearer and clearer in retrospect: the rise in Palestine of the socialist Zionist parties and their virtual monopoly over the basic institutions of the Jewish community in Palestine—called in Hebrew the *yishuv*.

Socialist Zionist parties began to be created almost immediately after the creation of the Zionist movement as a whole. But these parties were riven by the intense doctrinal divides common to the worldwide socialist movement since before Marx's time and intensified after his death. On the one hand were the orthodox Marxists (often but not always calling themselves communists), who advocated world revolution, the seizure of all private property and the means of production, and the creation of a dictatorship of the proletariat. On the other hand were the "utopian socialists" who believed in a peaceful road to socialism, the central role of the state in planning and running the economy, the nationalization of major industries and means of production, and the retention of private property and the democratic state.

The strictly Marxist form of socialist Zionism was propounded by the Ukrainian-born Ber Borokhov, who argued, on the basis of the teachings of dialectical materialism, that Jewish life in the Diaspora was unhealthy since its social structure resembled an "inverted pyramid": the vast majority of Jews in Eastern Europe were lower-middle-class traders and merchants, countered only by a tiny proletariat. Only in Palestine could that pyramid be turned on its head: the creation of a joint Jewish/Arab working-class majority in Palestine would necessarily engage in class warfare with both the Jewish bourgeoisie and the feudal Arab landlords. This class war would inevitably lead to a socialist revolution and hence true freedom for both the Jews and the Arabs of Palestine. This mélange of Marxism and Zionism became very influential in the Jewish community of Palestine in this period, though it met strong opposition on the part of the other, non-Marxist, socialist and Labor Zionist movements.

Though Weizmann's General Zionists dominated the movement in the Diaspora, in Jewish Palestine political life was overwhelmingly led by the leftist movements, along with the institutions they created, from the kibbutz, to the moshav, to the Histadrut Workers Union, to a communal healthcare system, a consumer distribution network, a school system, and even a socialist court system. Though the immigration of middle-class Jews challenged the hegemony of Marxist/socialist/Labor

Zionism, the latter held the reins of power throughout the interwar period.

However, in the 1920s and 1930s a major new force emerged within the Zionist movement in the Diaspora that challenged both the General Zionists and the left. This was the right-wing movement known as Revisionist Zionism, inextricably linked with its founder, Vladimir Jabotinsky. He was in many ways the opposite of the leaders and supporters of all previous Zionist movements since Herzl: born in the Russian Empire, he was raised in a Russified upper-middle-class family that had little if any Jewish content or connections, or any struggle with the push-and-pull between Jewish religious faith and modernity. After failing to make his mark as a Russian author, he turned to Jewish nationalism and moved from being a supporter of cultural Zionism to a more and insistent political Zionist.

His first major accomplishment in Zionist ranks was the creation of a Jewish fighting force—known as the Jewish Legion—within the British army in the First World War, and afterward moving to Palestine, where he was a central figure in the creation of the Haganah, the semi-legal fighting force of Labor Palestine. For this he was arrested and imprisoned by the British, and hence became a cause-célèbre and then a household name both in the yishuv and in Zionist circles in the Diaspora. Upon his release he returned to Eastern Europe and, unable to conduct Zionist activities in his homeland, now recast as the Soviet Union, he made his headquarters in Warsaw and traveled the Jewish world whipping up support for his increasingly right-wing vision of Zionism.

His first cause was opposition to the creation of Transjordan, denouncing it as a nefarious and illegal trick played by the British in violation of the Balfour Declaration and the Mandate, and condemning as treason the acquiescence of Weizmann and other Zionists in this "first partition of Palestine." His slogan "Two Banks of the River Jordan" became the rallying call of his supporters as he zigzagged in and out of the World Zionist Organization and eventually settled outside of it, in what he deemed a return to Herzlian political Zionism.

However, on social and economic grounds he was, in fact, further from Herzl than the socialist Zionists, espousing a blend of anti-socialist statism and more and more extreme right-wing nationalism, on the model of the East European proto-fascist movements rising in both Eastern and Western Europe in the 1920s and 1930s. Although he himself never crossed the line to full-fledged fascism (even though the Labor Zionist leader David Ben-Gurion dubbed him "Vladimir Hitler"), the youthful minions in his massively popular movement adopted the black-shirt uniforms of right-wing parties of the day, repeating his mantra that "all a Jewish boy needs to learn is to speak Hebrew and shoot a gun." He demanded that Jews reject the stereotypical demeanor of small-town Eastern European Jewry, cowering, cowardly, overly concerned with what either God (in whom Jabotinsky defiantly did not believe) or the Gentiles (whose attitudes he urged the Jews to emulate) would think about them. Instead, Jews should adopt an attitude he called *hadar*—roughly, aristocratic pride—a cool, unemotional, unyielding sense of dignity in one's bearing, mission, and national ethic. On this basis, most crucial was his strident opposition to any territorial or political concessions to the Arabs of Palestine; to his mind the Arabs had many other states in the Middle East that they could call their own, while the Jews were struggling to attain just one. His denial of the fundamental existence of the Palestinian nation and the legitimacy of its call for "autoemancipation" remained constant until his death in 1940, and is still held to this day among many of his followers in right-wing Zionist circles.

In the 1930s, however, as the economic and political situation of Jews in Eastern and Central Europe deteriorated in the face of rising anti-Semitism and Germany became ruled by the Nazis, Jabotinsky's right-wing nationalism found more and more support among Jewish youth in Poland and the Baltic States. In Palestine itself Revisionist Zionism had a far smaller presence, basically tethered to the growing but still relatively small middle- and lower-middle-class urban populations of the main cities.

By this time, all forms of Zionism had to face a far more life-threatening reality in its "national home": first, increased Palestinian violent resistance to the Zionist venture, culminating in a general strike in 1936 and all but continuous guerilla warfare against the yishuv, and, even more pointedly, the seeming reversal of British policy on Palestine, marked by "white papers" that all but rescinded the promise of a Jewish homeland contained in the Balfour Declaration. Britain seemed to be tilting in favor of the Arab population of Palestine and to the Arab states that could fulfill the need of the British Empire for oil. For one short moment the British raised the possibility of a truly radical solution to the "Palestine problem": the end of the Mandate and the partition of the country into Jewish and Arab states.

This proposal, advanced by the so-called Peel Commission in 1936, was reluctantly accepted by the mainstream of the Zionist movement, now led, along with Weizmann, by Ben-Gurion, the chair of the Jewish Agency for Palestine. It was, however, bitterly opposed by both the right and much of the left. The right rejected any partition of the Land of Israel. The anti-partition left was divided between the anti-statist socialist Zionists, led by the charismatic Berl Katznelson, who argued against what he called a version of the "Polish state" for the Jews in Palestine, and the Marxist left, which promoted a "binational" solution to the Arab-Jewish problem in Palestine.

In any event, the rejection of the very idea of partition by the Palestinian nationalist movement doomed the proposal to irrelevance, and Britain—led by its prime minister, Neville Chamberlain—moved formally to rescind the promise of the Balfour Declaration in the name of support for a joint

Arab-Jewish state and the limitation of Jewish immigration to Palestine to seventy-five thousand new immigrants over the next five years. In some ways, that last plank of this white paper hit home even more starkly than the others, since by the time it was issued, on May 23, 1939, the Jewish world was consumed by the horrors that had befallen the Jews of Germany and, more recently, those of Austria and Czechoslovakia, and the life-and-death danger to the rest of European Jewry caused by Nazi aggression.

Under this sword of Damocles, the Twenty-First Zionist Congress met in Geneva in late August 1939. Weizmann's policy of relentless support of Great Britain now seemed to have been not only mistaken but counterproductive, and his leadership role in the Zionist movement essentially came to an end. His last words to the Congress were: "I have no prayer but this: that we will all meet again alive." Two days later World War II broke out, and the fate not only of Zionism but of the Jewish people as a whole hung in the balance.

Chapter 6
Zionism in World War II and its aftermath

David Ben-Gurion's reaction to the 1939 white paper was at once more bellicose and more realistic than Weizmann's: "We will fight Hitler as if there were no White Paper, and the White Paper as if there were no Hitler." In reality, only the first plank of this policy was possible under the conditions that obtained after September 1, 1939: in total contrast to 1914 and 1917, when Weizmann was able to use the power (or, more precisely, the illusion of power) of world Jewry to support either side of the war, in 1939 there was no question of which side of the new world war the Jews would be on. The only Jews who opposed the Allies were the Communists who held to the party line after the Ribbentrop-Molotov pact of August 1939 and a tiny group of extreme right-wing Jewish terrorists who hated Britain more than the Nazis. But both in the Jewish world at large and within the Zionist movement in particular, support for the Allies' cause was unquestionable.

And so the Zionist movement at first focused on two all but contradictory goals: illegal immigration of Jews to Palestine against the policies of the Mandatory government and British armed forces, and a push to create a Jewish fighting force within the Allied ranks comparable to the Jewish Legion in World War I. Britain, to be sure, had little if anything to gain from a Zionist army in its midst, and much to lose, since the Palestinians were now playing the same game that Weizmann had played in 1917,

and they found much reason to support the Nazi cause: the hope
that a British defeat would lead to the end of the Mandate and
the Zionist presence in a postwar Palestine.

Moreover, large numbers of Jews in Palestine were volunteering
to fight in the British army without a specific Zionist unit, with
their goal being the total and absolute defeat of the Axis powers.
Indeed, Palestine itself was not immune from the threat of
Nazi invasion, as Rommel's forces advanced through Egypt.
Fortunately, his army did not succeed in reaching Palestine, and
the yishuv was spared the fate of its sister Jewish communities in
Europe. Only when the end of the war was nigh in September
1944 did Winston Churchill allow the formation of a "Jewish
Brigade" within the British army, more a symbolic gesture in the
wake of the news of the genocide of European Jewry than an act
of military exigency.

Apart from surreptitiously supporting illegal Jewish immigration
to Palestine, for the first two years of the war the Zionist movement
could do little but anxiously watch and wait, as the Axis forces
seemed to be unstoppable and more and more European Jews
came under their control. After the war, and especially as the
reality of the Holocaust came to be known, profoundly ahistorical
claims about what the Zionist movement should or could have
done to save European Jewry were broached. In reality, the Zionist
movement, and world Jewry at large, had virtually no political
power at all during the war years, save for the limited authority
over the yishuv exercised by the Jewish Agency. So attenuated was
this power that Ben-Gurion spent much of the war years outside
of Palestine, in London and increasingly in New York, as it became
clearer and clearer that the United States was becoming the most
important world power, along with the Soviet Union (which was,
crucially, at this point stridently opposed to Zionism and anything
reeking of Jewish nationalism among its huge Jewish population).
But Ben-Gurion's and Weizmann's lobbying efforts were severely,
limited by the fact that the Jewish community in the United States

could not have influenced Roosevelt's war policy even if it had
wanted to do so. The only real option left to American Jewry and
its leaders was to support the Allies as best they could, without
seeming to be advocating any parochial Jewish cause such as
Zionism, or, for that matter, intervention to save European Jewry
from annihilation. To be sure, behind the scenes influential
American Jewish leaders, Zionist and non-Zionist, tried to
influence their government's policy and make known the
unprecedented murder of Europe's Jews, but Roosevelt's
overarching goal of winning the war overruled any specific actions
for the benefit of the Jews—not to speak of American support
for Zionism after the war.

It is against this backdrop that a watershed moment in Zionist
history occurred in New York City in late May 1942, when a
Zionist conference at the Biltmore Hotel voted to make overt
and public what had been the unstated goal of most Zionists
heretofore: that after an Allied victory Palestine would be
established as a "Jewish commonwealth." The latter term was
largely, but not wholly, a euphemism for an independent state;
after all, in the American context four of the fifty states are
constitutionally "commonwealths." For the Weizmann supporters
at what came to be known as the "Biltmore Conference," the
ultimate goal was not necessarily total independence from
Britain but some sort of British consortium over autonomous
Jewish and Arab mini-states (sometimes called "cantons," after
the Swiss model). To Ben-Gurion and his supporters, this
was typical Weizmannian shilly-shallying: what the Jewish
people desperately needed was a sovereign Jewish state in
Palestine, period. Call it a "commonwealth" if that got more
votes at a meeting of diaspora Jews; reality would dictate the
inevitable result.

In truth, the Biltmore program received its importance only
retroactively; at the time, it was all but overwhelmed by the war
effort, and then slowly but unstoppably by the horrific news

emerging about the murder of six million European Jews. At first, the Zionist leadership, just like Jewish leaders everywhere, was reluctant to believe the stories smuggled out of the ghettos and death camps: they seemed, quite literally, unbelievable. But soon the reality hit home with a force unprecedented in the annals of Jewish responses to persecution. Perhaps the most enduring reaction to the Holocaust was theological: How could God have allowed six million Jews to be killed—not to speak of the God of Israel, who was believed to have chosen the Jews from "among all nations"? One profoundly understated poem by an American Yiddish poet raised as a Zionist in Eastern Europe, Kadya Molodowsky, began:

> O God of Mercy
> Choose—
> another people.
> We are tired of death, tired of corpses,
> We have no more prayers.
> Choose—
> another people.
> We have run out of blood.

Beyond the theological quandary, in the world of the here and now, by far the most important reaction to the Holocaust among Jews the world over was unprecedented support for Zionism: until 1945 Zionism was a small minority movement within the Jewish community, vociferously opposed by Orthodox and Reform rabbis alike, by emancipationist lay elites who believed in the integration of the Jews into the societies in which they lived, and by pragmatists who held that, whatever its worth as an ideal, Zionism was utterly impractical, especially given the opposition of the Palestinians, and indeed of the Arab world as a whole, to any such enterprise.

After 1945, internal Jewish opposition to Zionism began to disappear, increasingly relegated to the furthest extremes of small

Ultra-Orthodox cults or the tiny remnant of the antinationalist wing of the Reform movement.

Nothing could counter the indelible effect on Jewish sensibilities of the photographs and especially the newsreels of the death camps, the previously unimaginable but now all too brutally real images of masses upon masses of skeletons, dead and semi-living; the evidence of the crematoria; and the agony of the hundreds of thousands of Jews in Displaced Persons camps in Germany and elsewhere with no place to go. Although a large number of these refugees simply wanted to find a home anywhere they could be safe, the overwhelming majority of Jewish displaced persons, whatever their prewar political or religious affiliations, began to evince one goal and one goal alone: to go to Palestine to live in a Jewish state—a state that would not allow such a thing to happen again.

And so the official Jewish organizations in the West now supported the movement for a Jewish independent state in Palestine. Organizations such as the American Jewish Committee, B'nai B'rith, and the (Reform) Central Conference of American Rabbis now joined the cause.

The reality on the ground in Palestine, however, was hardly amenable to the Zionist cause. Both at the time and later, Jews and Arabs both claimed that the British were on the side of their opponents, and there is ample evidence to support each claim. And indeed, for the Zionists in Palestine after 1945 the second clause of Ben-Gurion's prewar call—to fight the white paper as if there were no Hitler—now came into play, although to be sure the battle against the British was joined with a battle on the ground against Arabs, now liberated as well from their wartime alliances to focus on defeating the Zionists and their plans to found a Jewish state on what they all but unanimously viewed as Arab land.

The real battle shifted to the cities, towns, and villages of Palestine itself. The Zionists were organized in four different "underground" forces: the Haganah, the fighting arm of Labor Zionism; its elite strike force, known as the Palmach; the Irgun (known in Hebrew as Ezel), the militant arm of the Revisionist movement, now headed by Menachem Begin after the untimely death of Jabotinsky in 1940; and the so-called Stern Gang (Lehi in Hebrew), an offshoot of the Irgun with more radical right-wing goals and openly terrorist tactics.

The Haganah—by far the largest group—at first struggled to sort out its disparate views on the fight against the British versus the Arabs and its relations with the Irgun. It ultimately settled on what it called a policy of "restraint"—that is, engaging only in self-defense operations rather than open guerrilla warfare against both of its opponents. The Palmach officially held to the same policy but maintained its own leadership based in the kibbutzim and their communitarian ethos, seeking far more avidly to attack British military targets with well-organized combat units. The Irgun wholeheartedly believed in a full-scale military campaign against both the British and the Arabs, with its most famous (or infamous) act being the bombing of the central offices of the Mandate in the King David Hotel in Jerusalem on July 22, 1946, in which ninety-one people were killed, mostly civilians.

Although Begin and others claimed that the hotel workers had been given ample warning to evacuate the building before the bombing and that the Haganah had been informed of the attack and coordinated backup support for the Irgun militants, this bombing came to symbolize the Jewish struggle against the British Mandate—though Ben-Gurion and other Haganah leaders insisted that they opposed such "terrorist" activities. The Lehi was committed to an all-out war against both the British and the Arabs, unconcerned with being labeled terrorists by Jews or Gentiles. Its most spectacular act before 1948 was the assassination of the British minister resident in Palestine, Lord Moyne, on November 6, 1944, ostensibly because of his opposition to the aims of the Zionist movement. But undoubtedly this was more an extraordinarily brazen display of the extent to which Jewish fighting forces could oppose their Gentile overlords.

Slowly but surely, the British government began to conclude that its position in Palestine was a lose-lose situation, that British soldiers, policemen, and civilians were dying for a cause that virtually no one on the home front could explain or defend. Although stalwarts like Churchill still believed that the British Empire could be saved and that British control over Palestine was a key to the empire's survival, more realistic voices in Whitehall and in the British public began to evince a view about the Palestine controversy summed up colloquially as "a plague on both your houses." At first, an Anglo-American Committee of Inquiry was set up to deal with the Palestine problem, with both sides concluding that neither the Jews nor the Arabs should found independent states on their own. But this quasi-alliance fell apart as a result of President Truman's call for one hundred thousand Jewish refugees to be admitted to Palestine immediately, something the British were steadfastly opposed to. And so in May 1947 Britain announced that it was handing over the Palestine problem to the newly formed United Nations, and that it would unilaterally terminate the Mandate over Palestine a year later, on May 15, 1948.

Quite naturally this led to frantic political machinations on the part of both the Zionist and the Palestinian leaderships. The latter made it absolutely plain that it would oppose ceding any territory of Palestine to the Jews, and had the entire Arab world behind this resolution. (The only exception was King Abdullah of Jordan, who tacitly was in favor of a compromise with the Zionists and met regularly, if secretly, with their leaders, though he was constrained from making any public declarations of support for their cause.)

Both in Palestine and in the Jewish diaspora, the overwhelming majority of Jewish and Zionist activists began to support the idea of partitioning Palestine into a Jewish state and an Arab state.

Opposition came from four radically different quarters: The Revisionists vocally opposed any territorial compromise whatsoever and held fast to their position of "both banks of the Jordan River." On the left, there was still substantial support for a binational state on the part of the Marxist Zionist movement, and the same idea was supported by the tiny, non-Marxist Ihud (Unity) party, a successor to the Brit Shalom movement of the 1930s, which leaned toward pacifism and included important intellectuals, largely of German origin, such as Martin Buber, Gershom Scholem, and Rabbi Judah Magnes, the chancellor of the Hebrew University of Jerusalem. In a dramatic display of dissent from the mainstream of the Zionist movement, both Buber and Magnes testified against partition before the United Nations Special Committee on Palestine in 1947, arguing for an economic union of Jewish and Arab "cantons" in Palestine. Finally, several members of Ben-Gurion's inner-circle cabinet supported the idea of partition but felt that the timing was not right for any proclamation of independence, given the dangers facing the yishuv of an armed attack by the Arab states neighboring Israel, in alliance with the local Palestinian forces.

Ben-Gurion's unwavering support for independence received crucial support from a totally unexpected quarter: the Soviet Union. In the midst of the General Assembly debate over the partition of Palestine, the Soviet ambassador, Andrei Gromyko, delivered a passionate speech that reversed his government's decades-long opposition to Zionism: while a binational state may be preferable in theory, Gromyko explained, the sufferings that the Jewish people had endured in the Second World War and the fact that no Western power had come to the aid of the Jews exterminated by Hitler (in sharp contrast to the actions of the Soviet Union), the Jewish people merited an independent state of their own in Palestine. In retrospect, it seems that Stalin was engaging in a simple exercise in realpolitik: with the British leaving the Middle East, a power vacuum would emerge, leaving an opening for Soviet influence and power. The Arab states were conservative monarchies led by kings and mullahs who were averse to the Soviet system. On the Zionist side, on the other hand, there was a significant pro-Soviet Marxist left which could be counted on to support whatever Stalin decreed, and a malleable non-Marxist but still socialist camp that could tilt the proposed new country if not totally into the Soviet camp then at least into the emerging group of "unaligned" countries such as India and Yugoslavia. In this way, the proposed Jewish state would be relied upon to side with the Soviets against the rising threat of American imperialism.

As a result of this Soviet shift of policy, when the General Assembly came to vote on the partition plan on November 29, 1947, not only the Soviet Union but also its client states Poland, Czechoslovakia, and the Belorussian and Ukrainian Soviet Socialist Republics voted in favor of partition, alongside the United States, other Western democracies, and most Latin American states. Without the Soviet Bloc, there would simply not have been enough votes to pass: by the strange rules of the General Assembly, a resolution required a two-thirds majority of the members present and voting (i.e., not counting abstentions). Thus, the partition plan required thirty-one yeas: it received thirty-three.

This vote sent most Zionists into a frenzy of joy; the longed-for Jewish state in Palestine was now within reach. However, two major obstacles stood in the way: first, in the months after the vote the United States began to backtrack from support for partition. Ben-Gurion and Weizmann used every trick in their playbook to counter this possible American about-face. On the other side of the debate, in an astonishing move Rabbi Judah Magnes made a secret trip to Washington in late April and early May 1948 to try to convince President Truman to oppose the imminent announcement of a Jewish state. By now Magnes was not really articulating the view of his Ihud party but was motivated by fear of massive bloodshed in the event of an Arab-Jewish war.

Indeed, the violence began immediately after the partition vote: at this point, there was essentially a civil war between the Palestinians and the Jews. But as the date of the British departure from Palestine—May 15, 1948—approached, it was clear that the Arab states neighboring Palestine would join the battle, with a result that no one could predict. In fact, fears about the inevitability of such a war found their way into the very center of the Zionist leadership of the yishuv. Ben-Gurion, of course, was the major proponent of the immediate declaration of independence on the very day that the British flag came down in Palestine for the last time. But even within his small cabinet, several members voted against declaring independence: the final vote was six for and four against. Just like the UN partition vote,

4. On May 14, 1948, as the British Mandate's armed forces were preparing to leave Palestine, David Ben-Gurion, the head of the Zionist proto-government, declaimed the Declaration of Independence of the State of Israel. It reflected Ben-Gurion's secular and socialist version of Zionism, with no mention of God or a divine promise of the Holy Land to the Jews.

then, the vote to establish the State of Israel was an extremely close call that could easily have gone the other way.

And so in the late afternoon of Friday, May 14, 1948, a few hours before the British Mandate for Palestine was set to expire at midnight, David Ben-Gurion hastily made plans for a history-making event, the culmination of the Zionist dream since 1897: a declaration of an independent Jewish state in Palestine, to be called the State of Israel.

On some level this was a strange name to be chosen for the new state: after all, in the Bible "Israel" was the name of the Northern Kingdom, the state that never truly transcended its paganism and thus lost out to the southern kingdom, "Judah," chosen by God. But Ben-Gurion's intuition was that a state named "Judah" or "the Jewish State" would not have the same resonance as "Yisrael," most significantly because of the millennial connection of that name to the Jewish people around the world—*am yisrael*—and to the Land of Israel: *erez yisrael.*

And so the Declaration of Independence of the State of Israel was read aloud in a solemn ceremony in Tel Aviv that Friday afternoon. Its text was rather hastily drafted and redrafted—the final version was revised so near to the time of the announcement that Ben-Gurion had to read it from a typed piece of paper, rather than the scroll that was ceremoniously signed afterward.

The text itself was a deft articulation of the secular, moderate, socialist Zionism of the majority of its signers, implicitly rejecting the views of Orthodox, Revisionist, and Marxist Zionists. Most cited in later decades was its vision of social justice and religious freedom: the state "will foster the development of the country for the benefit of all its inhabitants; it will be based on freedom, justice and peace as envisaged by the prophets of Israel; it will ensure complete equality of social and political rights to all its inhabitants irrespective of religion, race or sex; it will guarantee freedom of religion, conscience, language, education and culture; it will safeguard the Holy Places of all religions." Equally well-known, though often elided in official Israeli government translations of the declaration, was the deliberate and emphatic omission of the word "God" in the founding document of the Jewish state, since (once more) neither Ben-Gurion nor most of his colleagues believed in any traditional conception of a divinity. To appease the few Orthodox figures invited to sign the declaration, the drafters settled on the phrase *zur yisrael*—the Rock of Israel—which is one of the euphemisms used in Jewish liturgy for God, but could also be interpreted in non-theistic symbolic ways or even literally as the land of the Land of Israel.

Far less well known is the corollary to the God issue, perhaps even more radical in its bracingly secular Zionist ideology: the declaration made absolutely no mention of any divine promise of the Land of Israel to the Jews. Rather, it states that in the Land of Israel the Jewish people gave to the world the "Book of Books"—that is, the Bible was created by the Jewish people in their own land, not revealed by God to the Israelites at Sinai. And from that claim there followed a capsule history of the Jews as refracted through an unyielding Zionist lens: the Land of Israel was where the Jews as a people were founded and achieved political sovereignty. After losing their state and being exiled from their land, the Jews never ceased to pray for its revival; in recent generations they began returning to it as pioneers, and this movement led, in 1897, to the founding of the Zionist movement by Theodor Herzl. In other words, the Jews had no history in between 70 CE and Herzl, except for the hope to return to the Land of Israel.

This hope, the declaration continued, was made even more urgent by the murder of the Jews in World War II, and so the new state would immediately be open to unlimited Jewish immigration from around the world. And, knowing that the declaration of independence would inevitably lead to warfare with the Arab world, the declaration extended a call "to all neighboring states and their peoples in an offer of peace and good neighborliness," and appealed to them "to establish bonds of cooperation and mutual help with the sovereign Jewish people settled in its own land. The State of Israel is prepared to do its share in a common effort for the advancement of the entire Middle East."

Perhaps most fundamental was a simple statement near the end of the document that summarized the central plank of the Zionist movement from its prehistory in the modern Jewish nationalism of the 1870s: the right of the Jews to establish a state in their ancient homeland is "the natural right of the Jewish people to be masters of their own fate, like all other nations, in their own sovereign State."

Zionism had accomplished what Herzl had dreamed of when leaving the First Congress in Basel. And so, as the ink on the declaration was drying, the Union Jack was lowered for the last time at the residence of the British high commissioner for Palestine, replaced by the blue and white flag of the new State of Israel. That state braced itself for immediate war, and for the unprecedented challenges of actually creating and running a state rather than pining for one.

Chapter 7
Zionism in a Jewish state, 1948–1967

After the declaration of independence, the history of Zionism became entirely entangled with the history of the new State of Israel. While there still were a large number of Zionists in the diaspora, their role in the movement all but withered away, replaced by their political and financial support of the new state. Perhaps the most eloquent symbol of this shift was Ben-Gurion's sidelining of Weizmann in the weeks and days leading up to independence: the man who had led and epitomized Zionism for over three decades was not even present to sign the Declaration of Independence. He would, to be sure, later be named the first president of the state, but Ben-Gurion made sure that this office was essentially ceremonial and hence ephemeral.

But Zionism as an ideology did not cease to evolve after the creation of the state. Indeed, over the next decades both the realities and the hopes of the new state led to dramatic changes in its founding ideology.

First, during what the Israelis call the War of Independence from November 29, 1947, until the signing of armistice agreements in 1949, the Zionist state had to deal in a far more serious way than ever before with the reality that there were two nations fighting for sovereignty over the same land. And so the most controversial chapter of the history of the new State of Israel involves what precisely happened to the local Palestinian population during the battles that followed the establishment of the state. For decades, loyal Zionist historians steadfastly maintained that the Arab population had voluntarily fled from the towns and villages of Palestine, egged on by their leaders, who promised that they would all soon return to drive the Jews into the sea. Palestinian historians and their supporters maintained, in sharp contrast, that according to a preexisting plan, the Arabs were ruthlessly expelled from their land, violently evicted from their homes, and driven into exile in surrounding Arab countries in what became known as the "Nakba," the catastrophe.

While these two narratives persist to this day, on the Israeli side there has been in recent years a dramatic revision of the interpretation of 1948, acknowledging that Palestinians had indeed been expelled from various parts of the country. Even Israeli leaders such as Yitzhak Rabin have acknowledged in their memoirs expulsions from Lod and Ramle, and one of the canonical works of Israeli literature, S. Yizhar's *Khirbet Khizeh*, first published in 1949, deals with such an expulsion. The best objective evidence suggests that, as in so many massive flights of refugees in other war zones—the closest parallel is the population transfer that occurred in the wake of the creation of India and Pakistan just a year earlier—what happened in Israel was a combination of forced expulsions, panicked flight, and utter chaos. The upper classes of Palestinian society quickly fled the fight to places of safety within the Arab world and outside of it; the lower classes were caught between the Israeli desire to have as few Arabs as possible remaining in their new state and the Palestinians' desire to remain on the lands they regarded as their ancient national patrimony.

Fundamentally, what the Israeli leadership could not do for the first several decades of the state's existence was acknowledge that the central plank in their declaration of independence—that there exists "a natural right of every people to be masters of their own

fate, like all other nations, in their own sovereign state"—applied
to the Palestinians as well. Indeed, well into the late twentieth
century many Israeli leaders denied that there was, in fact, a
Palestinian nation. At the same time, the Palestinian leadership
refused to recognize the existence of a Jewish nation and its right
to sovereignty in Palestine.

This first challenge to Zionism in the new state was resolved by a
formal recognition of the equal rights of the Arab minority in
Israel in the Declaration of Independence, combined with the
imposition of military rule over Arabs in Israel that remained
in place until 1966. After the Six Day War of 1967 the "Arab
problem" became immeasurably sharpened, and *the* defining
issue of Israeli politics.

Meanwhile, in the early years of the state, a second goal of Zionism
took center stage: the "ingathering of the exiles." Immediately after
the declaration of the state, its gates were thrown open to Jews
from around the world, and within four years 687,624 arrived in
Israel, thus doubling its population from its pre-state high.

The government had not adequately prepared for the enormous
challenge of housing and feeding these immigrants, and with
almost no natural resources to call upon, Israel faced several years
of acute economic crisis while trying to absorb its new residents.
Moreover, the Zionist dream of Jews the world around quickly
moving to the new state had to be severely amended: the vast
majority of immigrants came from countries where the Jews were
persecuted and oppressed (sometimes because of their sympathies
with Zionism) or where economic circumstances prevented them
from living safe and fulfilling lives. Thus, Iraq and Romania
provided the largest numbers of Jews moving to Israel in its first
decade, and they were then joined by hundreds of thousands of
Jews from other Muslim or Communist countries. The true shock
to Zionism came from the reality of who did *not* come—the free
and successful Jewish communities of the Western world: North

5. Within four years of the establishment of the state of Israel in 1948, 687,624 Jewish immigrants arrived there from many places around the globe. Most—like the family in this photograph—arrived by boat at the port of Haifa and were then settled by the government in temporary housing until permanent quarters could be arranged for them.

America, Western Europe, Latin America, South Africa, Australia. Most crucially, by 1954 the Jewish community of the United States, the most important reservoir of political and financial support for the new state, numbered roughly five million people; in that year, a grand total of 349 Jews emigrated from the United States to Israel. In the first five years of Israel's existence, only 3,437 American Jews moved to Israel, roughly 0.5 percent of the total number of immigrants.

It took several years for Ben-Gurion and the other leaders of Israel to absorb this raw fact: while one of the planks of the Zionist idea was to serve as a safe haven for Jews in need, the other plank was a belief that the very existence of the state would impel Jews, even those in conditions of political freedom and economic stability, to move voluntarily to Israel, there to join in the grand Zionist experiment. That second plank had to be fundamentally rethought, as the same pattern obtained in the decades to come. Thus, when Morocco became independent of France in the early 1960s, most of its Jewish population elected to leave, but where they chose to go depended entirely on economic class: the richer Jews emigrated to France or Quebec, the poorer to Israel.

This points to another fundamental challenge to Israel's absorption of the new immigrants and thus the realization of the Zionist dream: the vast differences between Ashkenazic Jews and "Mizrachi" Jews—those from Muslim lands (often imprecisely called "Sephardim," a term which technically applies only to Jews who had their roots in the Iberian peninsula). While there were, to be sure, Sephardic and Mizrachi Zionists before 1948 (including an important group of Yemenite Jews who moved to Palestine at the start of the Zionist migration), they were a small minority of the Jewish population of Palestine and then Israel, and almost entirely absent from its leadership cadres. (Thus, only two Mizrachi figures signed the Declaration of Independence.) Moreover, Ben-Gurion and his minions were tied to a view of Jewish history based on the experience of the Jews in Europe, an expectation that once Jews were exposed to "modernity," they would undergo a fundamental transformation: First, they would shed their antiquated religious views and practices in favor of a new, secular worldview and style of life. Second, in that process they would shed the externalities acquired during "the Exile"—diasporic languages such as Yiddish, Ladino, or Judeo-Arabic and the cultures that were created in those exilic tongues.

In other words, Ben-Gurion and his colleagues took the model of European Jews to be the default position of world Jewry and ranked the Jews from the Mizrachi and Sephardic communities (as well as Ultra-Orthodox Ashkenazic Jews) as being culturally inferior, less successful beneficiaries of the process of "modernization" that was sweeping the whole world. They had to be remade into modern men even before they could be turned into

Israelis. This profound cultural bias combined with the economic crisis of the early years of the state meant that non-European Jews were housed in far inferior quarters than their Ashkenazic brethren (often in makeshift tent camps) and employed in lower-paying positions.

Moreover, the central idea of the ingathering of the exiles in the vision of Ben-Gurion and his colleagues, that these new immigrants would be utterly remade into true Israelis by the twin forces of the secular school system and the army, was in reality far more complex. From the start of the post-independence Mizrachi immigration, the religious Zionist parties in the parliament (now called the Knesset after the semi-mythical Great Assembly of ancient Judaism) and even in Ben-Gurion's own coalition vociferously objected to the fact that the children of these new immigrants were being sent to secular Zionist schools, as opposed to the parallel Orthodox Zionist school system that would respect their traditional religious beliefs and practices. Indeed, the frictions over this matter caused the first several crises of the new state, although in the end Ben-Gurion, as usual, got his way with minor concessions.

But even the religious Zionist parties did not dare challenge the hegemony of the Israeli army in transforming all immigrants—from Iraq, Poland, or South Africa—into a new type of Jew, not only trained into a superb military fighting force but also a bearer of the new Hebrew language, culture, and personality. Like the Sabra, the term for Jews born in Palestine/Israel, based on the prickly pear cactus of the same name, said to be spiny on the outside but soft on the inside, the Israeli soldiers would be hard as a rock externally, but humane and ethical at their core, unafraid to counter any enemy, never again cowering in the face of Gentile power, threats, or armed attack. The (alleged) example of the Jews in the Holocaust going to their deaths "like sheep to the slaughter" served as the most egregious counter-model to the new Israeli self-definition.

To be sure, no one at the time registered that this new Jew was gendered masculine, and it was unclear how women would fit into the Israeli ideal type. Already in September 1949 the Military Service Law included the mandatory conscription of women into the Israel Defense Forces with a slightly shorter term of service than men; Israel was the only country in the world with female conscription until Norway did so in 2015—and the North Korean government has announced a plan to do the same. How women would be treated in the army, whether they could fight in combat units, rise in the officer corps to top positions, and so on, slowly became major issues in the new state. More generally, in 1950 the Knesset passed a law on female equality that prohibited discrimination against women in any facet of life, while retaining the parliament's ability to pass laws treating women as women, most importantly in regard to maternity benefits. But this gender equality came with one big exception: laws of personal status regulating marriage, divorce, and adoption were vouchsafed to religious courts, in line with the old Ottoman practice that had been retained by the British Mandate. Thus, marriages, divorces, and other matters of "personal status" were to be determined by religious courts: for the Jews, rabbinical courts run exclusively by Orthodox rabbis; for Muslims, shariah courts; for Christians, various denominational courts; and Druze courts for the adherents of that religion. Although the details varied considerably among these faiths, in all cases women were discriminated against in matters of marriage and divorce.

But this was only one part—albeit a major one—of a series of concessions that Ben-Gurion and his Mapai party made to the non-Zionist (and anti-Zionist) Ultra-Orthodox parties in order for them not to argue against partition in the United Nations Special Committee on Palestine and the Anglo-American committees before the establishment of the state. These concessions are all part of the so-called status quo agreement Ben-Gurion made with the Agudat Yisrael in 1947—or at least this is what is widely believed to have happened, though a prominent Israeli scholar has called into question whether, in fact, such a compact was ever formally effected between the two sides.

In any event, the atheistic, secularist, moderate socialist Ben-Gurion did put into effect policies that not only assigned issues of personal status to religious courts but also promised that Saturday and Jewish holidays would be the officials days of rest in the new state; that food in the army, and ultimately in all state institutions, would be kosher; that Ultra-Orthodox Jews could have their own separate school system (alongside the state secular and Orthodox Zionist schools); and, seemingly incidental in the first years of the state, that young Ultra-Orthodox men studying in yeshivot (talmudic academies) would be exempt from military service. Ben-Gurion agreed to the last demand since he believed—or rather knew, at the depths of his being—that this was merely a temporary phenomenon, affecting only a few hundred young men, that as the state progressed and the inevitable process of secularization spread throughout the length and breadth of Israeli society, this quasi-medieval way of life would simply disappear and die out in the new, progressive Jewish state.

This concession on military service was the result, in addition, of a fateful decision Ben-Gurion made after the first election to the Knesset on January 25, 1949. Although it is all too often stated as an incontrovertible fact that from the start of the Israeli state there could not be a secular majority in the Knesset and hence the religious parties had to be brought into the coalitions, the simple numbers prove that this is absolutely not so: the Labor Zionist Mapai and Marxist Zionist Mapam together would have rendered 65 seats, an absolute majority in the 120-seat Knesset. And if Ben-Gurion had included in his coalition the other two Zionist secular parties, the Progressives and the General Zionists, that government would have controlled a solid 73 seats—thus having no need to make any concessions to the religious parties.

The simple reason why this did not happen was that the internecine hatreds, squabbles, and splits in the Israeli left were so profound and so intense that they could not be breached; the debates over Marxism versus the ideology of A. D. Gordon, the split in the kibbutz movement between those affiliated with the Social Democratic Mapai and the Marxist Mapam; the profound gulf between Mapam's unquestioning support of the Soviet Union versus Mapai's slow but insistent creep into the pro-American camp of the emerging Cold War; and, finally, the intense personal hatreds among socialist Zionists led Ben-Gurion to prefer a coalition that included the United Religious Front as well as the Progressives and General Zionists and not Mapam.

The one party that Ben-Gurion hated even more than Mapam was the right-wing Herut Party, led by Menachem Begin. Before the war, the Labor Zionists and Revisionists entered into pacts to try to combine their forces against the British, but the animosity between the two rivaling ideologies and movements was relentless and intense. Ben-Gurion did not invite Begin to attend the signing of the Declaration of Independence on May 14, 1948, or to attach its name to it as one of the founders of the state. But by far the most important altercation between the Labor Zionists and the Revisionists occurred soon after the establishment of the state. Ben-Gurion had insisted that all the independent fighting forces of Jewish Palestine be consolidated into the newly formed Israel Defense Force (IDF), essentially modeled on the Haganah. This was opposed by the Palmach, which was based in the kibbutzim and had its own, communitarian culture, and also by the Irgun and the Lehi. In the early months of 1948, the Irgun had secretly arranged for a large shipment of arms donated by the French government to be brought to Palestine for its use in the ongoing War of Independence. The departure of the boat, manned by 940 volunteers and named *Altalena*, one of Jabotinsky's pseudonyms, was delayed, and it arrived off the shore of Israel during the first ceasefire in mid-June between the IDF and the Arab armies. Begin seems not to have known of the timing of this arrival, but as it was approaching the coast of the newly formed Israel, he entered into frenzied negotiations with Ben-Gurion about how many of the weapons would be retained by the Irgun and how many handed over to the IDF. Ultimately, Ben-Gurion insisted that the retention of an independent, ideologically based "army within an army" was impermissible in any modern state. As the Altalena arrived at the shores of Israel, Begin rejected Ben-Gurion's ultimatum to surrender, and IDF troops fired at the ship, setting it aflame. In the end, thirty-two Irgun fighters and two IDF soldiers were killed.

The two sides—and particularly the two leaders—never forgave each other. To Ben-Gurion, Begin was a proto-fascist and a potential fomenter of civil war in the fragile new state. To the end of his days he refused to mention Begin by name. For his part, Begin blamed the whole fiasco on Ben-Gurion's lust for power and willingness to shed even Jewish blood for his nefarious purposes.

The delegitimization of the Revisionist Zionists, now the Herut Party, went much further than Ben-Gurion's personal quirks. The Labor Party ran the major bases of power in the young state, from the army and the Knesset, to the Histadrut Labor Federation (through which an enormous number of jobs were allocated to citizens), to the major consumer outlets and manufacturing plants. Being out of this loop was a distinct disadvantage, economically and socially, in the first decades of Israel's existence. Many well-known academics who were Revisionist Zionists could not obtain appointments at the Hebrew University, also under control of the Labor establishment.

Events soon led Begin and Herut as a whole to be regarded even more as outcasts in the political life of the country. In 1952 the Ben-Gurion government announced that it had entered into negotiations with West Germany to receive reparations for the murder of the six million Jews in the Holocaust. To Ben-Gurion and his supporters, not only was this morally just—the Israeli government regarded itself as the rightful heir to the European Jews who were exterminated—but it was also just that funds from Germany would allow Israel to accomplish its major new goal, absorbing the millions of Jews coming home to the Jewish state. He was well aware that there was an inevitable aura of unsavoriness to this deal, that the German term *Wiedergutmachung*—"making things good again"—could be read as relieving the German people of its responsibility for the genocide of the Jews. But to Ben-Gurion, the desperate state of Israel's economy and the righteous nature of the "ingathering of the exiles" overshadowed and overcame any hesitancy on his part.

But not to Begin and the other Herut leaders, who viewed the reparations agreement as an utter betrayal of the millions of martyred Jews of Europe, "blood money" which Israel was forbidden to accept—unto death. As the Knesset was debating the issue, Begin led a fiery protest that called for a violent overthrow of the government and its immoral prime minister. In the end, the putsch never occurred, the reparations bill was passed, and Begin was removed from the Knesset for three months. But for the next fifteen years (from 1952 to 1967) Herut as a party and Revisionist Zionism as an ideology were relegated to the margins of Israeli life and politics.

The extent to which the Mapai-led government actually implemented any form of socialism in the first decades of Israel's existence has been fiercely debated. Certainly, Israel instituted all the basic features of a European welfare state: free education and healthcare, subsidized prices for basic food wares as well as housing; a strong nationwide labor union that controlled a huge portion of the employment market. On the flip side, while a proto–stock market had already been created in Palestine in 1935, in 1953 a full-scale stock exchange was set up in Tel Aviv, even though the number of businesses large enough to become joint-stock companies was very small. There were, however, a growing number of small, family-owned shops, artisan workplaces, and small retail businesses in a growing capitalist sector of the economy that had not been envisioned by the founders of Labor Zionism.

The most successful manifestation of socialism remained the kibbutzim, which provided a large number of major political and military leaders. The Marxist-based kibbutzim still practiced communal ownership of the means of production and raising of children. But as the years passed, the absolute prohibition of private property was moderated, as more and more small-scale property was permitted for members—at first, their own clothes, a radio, a phonograph, possibly a kitchen in which to prepare small meals. And in the kibbutzim affiliated with Mapai rather than Mapam, children began more and more to be housed with their parents, responding to the latter's demands that a nuclear family was a natural component of humanity rather than a locus of social pathology and errant bourgeois individualism.

On a deeper level, what the kibbutzim, and the socialist ideology they maintained, imparted to Israeli society was an unyielding belief that the collectivity was the ultimate arbiter of behavior rather than the individual, whose unique talents, skills, and even hopes and aspirations had to be directed toward the collective. In earlier periods, the collectivity was defined variously as the Jewish people, the yishuv, the party, class. Increasingly, this collectivity was redefined as the state, and a neologism was invented to articulate this new stance: *mamlachtiyut*, best translated as étatism. Though, to be sure, Israeli citizens (or at least Jewish Israeli citizens) enjoyed the rights enumerated in the Declaration of Independence, in practice these rights were often subordinated to the good of the state.

Perhaps most exemplary of this reality was the issue of a constitution: in the Declaration of Independence, a promise was made that a constitution "shall be adopted by the Elected Constituent Assembly not later than the 1st October 1948."

However, this date came and passed without even the hint of a constitution, replaced by a compromise that the Knesset would gradually pass important legislation that would incrementally result in a constitution-like law code. Most often, the responsibility for the failure to pass a constitution has been laid at the feet of the religious parties, which insisted that any constitution for a Jewish state must be guided by the principles of the Torah and traditional Jewish law, something that was repugnant to the secular majority of the new state. While this was indeed a serious obstacle to any agreement over a constitution, the far more central reason for the lack of one was Ben-Gurion's intuition that any constitution would constrain his power as prime minister and his ministers' executive powers over all aspects of the new state. At the same time, Ben-Gurion rigorously argued that the concept and practice of judicial review central to the workings of the US Supreme Court were antidemocratic, in that they overturned laws drafted by the democratically elected legislature. But clearly his overarching goal was to ensure the greatest amount of power vouchsafed to the prime minister and his ministers.

Perhaps the most important arena where the reality of statehood departed radically from the ideological goals of pre-state Zionism was in that of foreign policy. Herzl had argued in *The Jewish State* that in that state "the generals would be kept in their barracks," and none of the pre-state ideologues (including Jabotinsky) seriously grappled with the notion that a sovereign state would require not only a standing army but also a clear foreign policy. Already during the War of Independence the generals and the high officers of the IDF were not confined to their barracks—they were hugely influential in both planning and executing the military strategy, tactics, and day-to-day actions of the army, and after the war they became important leaders in the country's political life. In regard to foreign policy, the leftist parties of the Israeli political spectrum—not just the Communist Party but also Mapam (and at times the party known as Ahdut HaAvoda, Unity of Labor) were steadfastly loyal to the Soviet Union and its Cold

War realpolitik. Although some influential figures in Mapai and other non-Marxist socialist Zionist parties argued that Israel should remain neutral in the battle between the United States and the Soviet Union, Ben-Gurion insisted that Israel's future lay in a tight alliance with the Western nations and against the Soviet bloc, and in this he was supported by the centrist, religious, and right-wing parties.

The first and most controversial outcome of this alliance was the debacle of the Suez Campaign in 1956, when Israel secretly plotted with France and Britain to mount an attack on Egypt; the goal was to "liberate" the Suez Canal for its former owners and for Israel to gain control over the Gaza Strip and the Sinai Peninsula in order, ostensibly, to prevent the large number of cross-border raids by Egyptian and Palestinian militants. To what extent Ben-Gurion and his military advisers truly wanted to gain permanent control over these territories is a matter of keen debate among historians. And although the IDF was very successful in mounting its air and land campaigns against the Egyptians, Israel was forced by international pressure, particularly the American government (which regarded this whole campaign as illegal and ill-conceived) to withdraw from all territories it had conquered. After this debacle Israel continued to forge a close link with France, but its leaders began a massive effort to court favor in Washington. Zionism seemed now to be ineluctably tied to the ideology of liberal capitalism, as opposed to socialism, and to a foreign policy on the side of the West against the Soviet Union.

Finally, in these years a major development occurred in the realm of domestic politics: the battle over the question "Who is a Jew?" From the start of modern Jewish nationalism in the 1870s, Jewishness was redefined as a nationality rather than a religion; one could be a Jew and then a Zionist while believing, or not believing in, God; following or not following God's commandments; even, in theory, adhering to another religion while defining oneself as a member of the Jewish nation. Most famously, the second most important leader of the early Zionist movement, Max Nordau, never asked his Protestant wife or daughter to convert to Judaism—Why should they take on a religion I do not believe in, he asked?—while remaining loyal and active Zionists. Soon thereafter, the daughter of none other than Eliezer Ben-Yehuda married a German Protestant living in Jerusalem who was an avid believer in the Zionist cause and especially in the revival of the Hebrew language. Similarly, in the early 1930s the great Hebrew and Zionist poet Shaul Tchernikhovsky immigrated to Palestine along with his Christian wife and children; although there were some murmurs of discomfort with this break from Judaism, Tchernikhovsky's fame as the second national poet after Hayim Nahman Bialik trumped any opposition to his mixed-religion family. Finally, one of Vladimir Jabotinsky's right-hand men was Colonel John Patterson, a British officer who became the commander of the Zion Mule Corps and then of part of the Jewish Legion; after the war he remained very active in the Zionist movement, serving as a crucial part of fundraising missions in the United States. He was adulated by many—and especially right-wing—Zionists who reveled in the fact that he was a non-Jew rather than questioning whether a non-Jew could be part of the Zionist movement.

After the State of Israel was founded, one of its earliest and most important actions was passing the Law of Return in 1950. After very spirited debate, the substantial secular majority in the Knesset rejected Orthodox demands to define Jews by traditional Jewish law, which held that only children of a Jewish mother and those who converted to Judaism under Orthodox law were Jewish. The Law of Return deliberately left the word "Jew" undefined in the legislation, which began: "Every Jew has the right to come to this country as an immigrant."

At first, this did not pose much of a problem, since the majority of the new migrants came from countries where intermarriage between Jews and non-Jews was rare; the few non-Jewish spouses (usually wives) and children were simply registered as Jews by clerks who felt that they were upholding the law as stated. However, after the 1956 Polish uprising and its complex aftermath for that country's Jews, some sixty thousand left Poland and immigrated to Israel. Given the extremely high rates of intermarriage in Communist Poland, it was inevitable that a good number of these new immigrants would have non-Jewish spouses and children.

For the first time, Zionism as an ideology had to face the real-life implications of its definition of the Jews as a nation and not a religion. Ben-Gurion was convinced that these non-Jewish spouses and children could and should be accepted as part of the Jewish people. In a letter to "Jewish scholars" around the world, Ben-Gurion argued that in the Diaspora intermarriage resulted in "assimilation," or the loss of families to the Jewish people. But in Israel, he insisted, the reverse was true: non-Jewish spouses and children melded into the society and body politic of the Jewish state and indeed strengthened it. In sharp contrast, almost all the scholars he wrote to insisted he was dead wrong, that the Jewish state had to maintain the traditional Jewish matrilineal definition of who is a Jew, in order to keep the Jewish people united worldwide.

Matters came to a head with the arrival in Israel of Oswald Rufeisen, a Polish Jew who had been an active Zionist in prewar Poland, fought against the Nazis and saved Jews, and voluntarily converted to Catholicism during the war, in turn becoming both a monk and a priest. But he remained a Zionist and joined the Carmelite monastic order, since its headquarters were on Mount Carmel in Haifa. When finally allowed to leave Poland in 1958, Brother Daniel, as he was now called, arrived at the port of Haifa wearing his long brown friar's cassock with a huge crucifix on his chest, declaring his intention to become a citizen of the Jewish state as a Jew by nationality and a Catholic by religion. Not surprisingly, the immigration officer denied the request. Rufeisen pursued his case all the way to the Supreme Court. Here, one of the ironies was that those who wanted the Jewish state to be governed by traditional Jewish law (halachah) had to admit that Brother Daniel was, indeed, a Jew; both of his parents—and, crucially, his mother—were Jews; and although there were minority opinions to the contrary, the overwhelming rabbinic holding over the centuries was that Jews remain Jews even after converting to another faith.

In fact, none of the justices on the Supreme Court believed that traditional Jewish law should govern the new state. The problem was rather whether the new state could actually accept as a Jew a practicing and believing Christian who so blatantly insisted on his right to be a Jew and a Christian, a Zionist and a Catholic friar. The majority of the justices concluded they simply could not: one did not have to be a believing Jew to be a Jew in the new Zionist state, but one could not uphold another religion.

For Israel as a whole, and Zionism at its ruling ideology, the "Who is a Jew?" debate continued to eat away at the consensus of what it meant to be a Jew in a secular Jewish state and, far more broadly, that state and society had to grapple with the relationship between Jewish nationalism and the Jewish religion in a way that the founders of Zionism could never had imagined. Even Vladimir Jabotinsky was famously antagonistic to religion: in his will he wrote that he did not care if he was buried or cremated, only that his remains be brought to an independent Jewish state—thereby contravening the absolute prohibition of cremation in Jewish law. But the overarching question of the relationship between Zionism and Judaism would be dramatically reframed in the wake of the Six Day War of June 1967.

Chapter 8
Nationalism and messianism, 1967–1977

In 1964, a major symbolic affair took place in Jerusalem: the new prime minister, Levi Eshkol, a stalwart veteran of Mapai, permitted the reinterment in Jerusalem of the remains of Vladimir Jabotinsky, who had died in 1940 in New York State. A state funeral was held for Jabotinsky, who was then buried with full military rites at Mount Herzl, the burial place of the heroes of Zionism from Herzl on.

One hundred miles away, in the bucolic desert enclave of Sde Boker where he made his home, David Ben-Gurion seethed: he had fought bitterly against Jabotinsky for decades, despising his ideology that married militarism and antagonism to any partition of Palestine with an unyielding anti-socialist, pro-capitalist, anti–labor union economic and social policy. At the time, though, the state burial of Jabotinsky seemed to be a rather minor affair, Eshkol's attempt to rectify a rather petty historical wrong and, in the process, to lower the animosity between Mapai and Herut.

In retrospect, however, it looms large as the first stage in two intertwined historic developments: the dilution of the socialist component of Mapai's Labor Zionism in favor of a more centrist economic and social politics, and the de-marginalization and ultimate embrace of Herut as a party and of Begin as its leader as full members of Israel's political establishment.

These developments occurred as seemingly minor side issues in the most consequential event in Israel's history in the second half of the twentieth century, its victory in the Six Day War of June 1967 and consequently its occupation of the West Bank, the Golan Heights, the Gaza Strip, the Sinai Peninsula, and East Jerusalem.

Dozens of books and articles have been written about this war and its outcome: some laud the military genius of Israel's victory, while others proclaim it a miracle wrought by God in returning Biblical lands to the Jewish people. Still others maintain that Israel's preemptive strike on the Arab forces was merely an excuse for launching a preplanned territorial aggression against Palestinian lands and the Palestinian people, in the name of a vicious colonial policy of the aggrandizement of the Zionist state at all costs.

Relevant here is, first, the Middle Eastern context: in late May and early June 1967, the pressure mounted on Eshkol to respond to Egyptian president Nasser's closing of the Straits of Tiran to Israeli ships, a move regarded by Israel and much of the world community as an act of war. Eshkol—a vacillator by nature—decided to yield to pressure and form a national unity government that would lead the nation in this crisis. To this end, he invited Moshe Dayan, the hugely popular former IDF chief of staff, to be minister of defense and Menachem Begin to be minister without portfolio. With the appointment of Begin to the cabinet, the deep rift in the Zionist movement since the 1920s between the Revisionists and the socialist Zionists was healed. And unlike the burial of Jabotinsky, this appointment had real-life consequences as the bellicose Begin (and Dayan) steadfastly supported a preemptive strike and an aggressive military defeat of the Arab states.

Israel's full-scale preemptive strike on both Egypt and Syria on June 5, 1967, was far more successful than anyone had anticipated, and within the next few days, a complete victory was

6. During the Six Day War of 1967, Israel Defense Force paratroopers advanced through the Old City of Jerusalem and reached the Western Wall, the most important symbol of Judaism, on June 7. The photograph of these three soldiers became the iconic image of the conquest of Jerusalem. It is especially noteworthy that the middle soldier is not covering his head at this holy site, a potent symbol of Zionist secularism.

at hand. But one huge part of this story is sometimes forgotten in the retelling of the Six Day War: that Israel's occupation of the West Bank and East Jerusalem was made possible by what King Hussein of Jordan later called "the worst mistake of my life." He had been in constant communication with the Israeli government in the preceding years and had pledged not to participate in a war should one break out, even though he had signed a mutual defense pact with Egypt. After the first days of the war he succumbed to the blandishments of Nasser to join the fray and committed his forces to engage with the IDF in East Jerusalem and throughout the West Bank. Though his well-trained forces provided a much more forceful rebuff to the Israeli military than those of Egypt and Syria, in the end Jordan lost control of East Jerusalem and the West Bank to Israel.

Had Hussein kept to his word and stayed out of the war, the history of Israel, of Zionism, of the Palestinians, of the Mideast, and indeed of the world, would have been entirely different.

Virtually all segments of Israeli society were deliriously happy after the country's massive success on the battlefield, and they reveled in a triumphalism not felt before in the history of the young state. One example from popular culture will illustrate this point: just before the Six Day War broke out, the songwriter and singer Naomi Shemer introduced a song called "Jerusalem of Gold," which bemoaned the partitioning of the capital since 1948, including the following verses:

> How the cisterns have dried
> The market-place is empty
> And no one frequents the Temple Mount
> In the Old City.
> And in the caves in the mountain
> Winds are howling
> And no one descends to the Dead Sea
> By way of Jericho.

Immediately after the conquest of East Jerusalem, Shemer updated the lyrics:

> We have returned to the cisterns
> To the market and to the market-place
> A ram's horn calls out on the Temple Mount
> In the Old City.
> And in the caves in the mountain
> Thousands of suns shine
> We will once again descend to the Dead Sea
> By way of Jericho!

This song quickly became the anthem for the war, both in Israel and in the Diaspora, but very few Israelis or foreign Jews paid heed to the fact that the original lyrics were blatantly inaccurate: the market of East Jerusalem was not devoid of people before June 6, 1967—in fact it was buzzing with huge crowds; thousands upon thousands of people did ascend the Temple Mount every week; and many descended to the Dead Sea via Jericho. However, before June 1967 these people were Arabs, not Jews, and thus invisible (or eradicated) in Shemer's nationalist imagination, now more and more shared by Israelis across the political spectrum.

Thus, Zionism in Israel and abroad had to embrace a new and highly complicated reality: the sudden rule by the Israeli army over approximately one million Palestinians—roughly six hundred thousand in the West Bank and East Jerusalem and another four hundred thousand in the Gaza Strip. It is inarguable that the vast majority of citizens of the State of Israel as well as almost all of its political leaders viewed this situation as temporary, assuming that the territories gained in the war (with the exception of East Jerusalem, which the Israeli government quickly annexed) would be exchanged in a peace treaty that would finally solidify the boundaries and the security of the Jewish state. Even Ben-Gurion, hardly a wilting flower when it came to territorial expansion, publicly called for the prompt return of all of the occupied territories except for East Jerusalem. (After a quick helicopter tour of the north, he added the Golan Heights as well, convinced that they were crucial to secure Israel from further attack by the Syrian army.)

Indeed, ever since late June 1967, virtually all public opinion polls of the Israeli population on the question of the occupied territories report a solid majority of Israelis in favor of returning the West Bank in exchange for peace. It is the next question in the polls that always yields the most important brake on that majority view: To whom should Israel cede these territories? Is there "a partner for peace," as the Israeli cliché has it?

Crucial here is the effect of the conquest of these territories on Zionism, as the occupation of the territories in the 1967 war slowly became the "new normal" for much of Israel. A country that regarded its struggle as a David versus Goliath, a tiny and insecure state surrounded by enemies, now felt vastly more secure, buffered by the territory it had conquered. But soon, a different element entered into the equation: three separate ideological forces (or three new iterations of Zionism) which supported, called for, and manned Jewish settlements in the Occupied Territories, in what one analyst has called an "accidental empire."

First, it is crucial to understand that it was not Begin's Herut party or the Orthodox Zionists that presided over the beginnings of the settlement movement: the first settlements occurred under the auspices of the Labor governments of the early and mid-1970s, as a result both of acquiescence in on-the-ground actions of the radical Orthodox right and developments within the Labor Zionist ranks themselves. The Ahdut HaAvoda wing of socialist Zionism, represented in the Israeli government by Yigal Allon, had always merged territorial expansionism with a socialist Zionism to the left of Mapai. Soon, Allon became the most important exponent of creating Jewish settlements along the Jordan River, thus ensuring the defense of Israel against attacks from the east; this plan was therefore dubbed the "Allon plan." Although it was not implemented in full (it included bizarre elements such as an autonomous Druze mini-state in the north), a good number of settlements were indeed set up in the areas designated by Allon and in other parts of the West Bank by the Labor governments in the decade after 1967.

The second group, founded soon after the war, was a new secularist movement called the Greater Israel Movement (Erez yisrael ha-shelemah). This group included well-known former leftist political and literary figures, who declared that not one inch of the territory of the occupied land could be given back in any peace agreement. While this group had important ideological influence in post-1967 Israel, its efforts on the ground were far less extensive than the third, and most important, group of exponents of the settlement policy: a radical new variation on Zionism and on Jewish messianism within the National Religious Party, the Gush Emunim ("bloc of the faithful"), which changed the face of Israel in a way not predicted by anyone.

By 1967, the original opposition to Zionism on the part of the vast majority of Orthodox rabbis and laity had all but lapsed. A radical extreme Ultra-Orthodox fringe group retained its virulent anti-Zionism, while the mainstream Ultra-Orthodox groups made their peace with the Jewish state, voted in its elections, served in its parliament, and even served as ministers of the realm. The religious Zionist movement remained solidly ensconced as representing roughly 10 percent of the population and enunciating a moderate political stance closely tied to the Labor Party.

Largely under the surface, however, a formidable messianic ideology was brewing at the very core of Orthodox Zionism. This was the brainchild of Rabbi Abraham Isaac Kook, who was born in 1865 in the Russian Empire and served in various minor rabbinical positions in Eastern Europe before immigrating to

Palestine in 1904 to become the chief rabbi of Jaffa. In 1921 he assumed the position of the Ashkenazi chief rabbi of Palestine.

Given Kook's cooperation with the Zionist authorities, many assumed that he was a supporter of Mizrachi. However, he was never a Zionist, although he advocated working closely with the secular Zionists in their efforts to return Jews to the Holy Land. What was actually at play, however, was a profound, dense, and highly esoteric mystical theology. For Kook, the secular Zionists were unconsciously doing God's work by returning to the Holy Land and building its communities and institutions. The secular Zionists' ideological and religious viewpoints were thus irrelevant to the process of the redemption of the Jewish people to which they were contributing.

Kook's messianism was entirely theoretical, but soon the subterranean messianic tension latent in his teachings bred a far more overt and activist theology in the ranks of his students. Led by his son, Rabbi Zvi Yehuda Kook, this ideology advanced an interpretation of Rabbi Kook's thought in which the conquest of the Holy Land was regarded as a divine act heralding the advent of the messianic age, "quickly and in our day," as the liturgy had traditionally put it.

In the years before 1967, this radical theology became more and more popular among younger National Religious Party activists, who founded Gush Emunim, which put forth an entirely unprecedented variation on Jewish messianism: a messianic movement without a messiah. The only parallel to this phenomenon was one that would shock the adherents of Gush Emunim: the Reform movement's rejection of a personal messiah in the name of the realization of the vision of the prophets of Israel.

Gush Emunim's radical innovation was that the land of the Land of Israel itself substituted for a personal messiah; the "redemption" of any of its land would inexorably lead to the "end of days." Followers of Gush Emunim began to create small and, at the beginning, illegal settlements in the West Bank, challenging the government to uproot them. Although the governments did attempt at the start and sporadically later to abolish these outposts, as the years progressed more of these settlements were founded, both by Gush Emunim and by other groups. More broadly, a significant segment of secular Israeli society began to feel that these new settlers, Orthodox or not, were the closest anyone in Israel had come in decades to the early pioneers of Zionism who sacrificed the comforts of their previous lives out of a "pioneering spirit" that had evaporated in recent decades.

Slowly, the number of Jewish settlements in the West Bank, the Golan Heights, and Sinai multiplied, as did Jewish neighborhoods created in East Jerusalem. Still, the Labor governments remained committed to a policy of land for peace.

At this time, on another front, a different phenomenon began to seriously affect the history of Zionism and of Israel: the mass immigration of Jews from the Soviet Union. This was made possible first by a significant change in the Law of Return, passed by the Knesset in 1970. The new law read: "The rights of a Jew under this Law and the rights of an [immigrant] under the Nationality Law, 5712–1952, as well as the rights of an [immigrant] under any other enactment, are also vested in a child and a grandchild of a Jew, the spouse of a Jew, the spouse of a child of a Jew and the spouse of a grandchild of a Jew, except for a person who has been a Jew and has voluntarily changed his/her religion." This amendment was passed primarily to respond to several controversial Supreme Court decisions regarding the question of who is a Jew, but it had revolutionary consequences for the third largest Jewish community in the world, that of the Soviet Union. In the middle and late 1960s there had occurred a small resurgence of Zionism and Judaism in the Soviet Union, parallel to the movements calling for civil and human rights in the country. The American Jewish community responded by organizing a drive to "save Soviet Jewry," convincing the US government to tie the sale of vital technology to the Soviet Union to the release of Jews seeking to emigrate. The Soviet government grudgingly responded by allowing an unprecedented number of Jews to emigrate. Some of the Jews who left the Soviet Union elected to move to the United States or other Diaspora countries, but the majority moved to Israel. Not all of these new immigrants were Zionists, and most were from territories that had been annexed to the Soviet Union since 1945 or were from the Caucasus or Muslim regions that had not gone undergone the processes of "dejudaization" experienced by Jews in the Russian, Belorussian, and Ukrainian republics. Thus, from 1968 to 1979 almost 250,000 Jews came to Israel from the Soviet Union.

The country they came to, however, changed radically under their feet, as a result of yet another war—the Yom Kippur War of 1973, in which the armies of Egypt and Syria launched a surprise attack on Israel that led to major military successes; only after a few days did the IDF and the political leadership rebound from their shock and successfully repel their enemies. But Israel's military victories were not matched by political ones: on the contrary, the leadership of Prime Minister Golda Meir and Minister of Defense Moshe Dayan was broadly condemned by the Israeli public. An investigative commission led by Supreme Court Justice Agranat formally absolved Meir and Dayan from direct responsibility, placing blame on the IDF leadership, but Meir and Dayan never regained the trust or support of the public and resigned from office barely seven months after the war ended.

In retrospect, five new developments in the history of Zionism resulted from the Yom Kippur War: First, the widespread triumphalism in the wake of the Six Day War was severely, if not critically, punctured by the military failures of the first days of the Yom Kippur War. To many, Israel once more seemed a fragile state always on the brink of extinction. Second, emigration *from* Israel increased, although still in small numbers, and gradually lost the sharp stigma attached to it in Israeli society and culture. More and more Israelis began to have a brother, a sister, and increasingly a child who left Israel for the West. In short order, both New York and Los Angeles would have enormous communities of émigré Israelis, and ultimately and most confusingly for Israeli and Zionist ideologies, some Israelis moved to Berlin and other cities in Germany. As the decades wore on, the question of what Zionism could mean to Jews who were born and bred in Israel but voluntarily left it for an easier life not marked by constant warfare and economic crisis emerged as a keen challenge to the core of Zionism.

Third, in the immediate aftermath of the Yom Kippur War, a reserve captain in the IDF who had been the commander of a major outpost during the war set up camp outside the prime minister's office in Jerusalem with a sign that read: "Grandma, your defense is a failure, and three thousand of your children are dead." While, of course, Israel and before that the Zionist movement had had a substantial number of bitter internal controversies, this protest by an apolitical army officer accusing the prime minister and her government of direct responsibility for the failure of the war and the deaths of thousands of soldiers was unprecedented, and it garnered substantial support. In due course, this protest would grow exponentially into the Peace Now movement and other NGOs whose basic raison d'être was opposition to the Occupation, to the settlements, and to the policy of any government, left- or right-wing, that supported them.

The fourth new development was a decline of Israel in the international community, resulting from two separate but connected factors: mounting criticism of the occupation of the West Bank and Gaza and hence the rise of support for the Palestinian cause, particularly in the developing world, and

7. Founded in 1978, Peace Now (Shalom Akhshav) was one of the largest antiwar and anti-Occupation movements in Israel. This poster reads "To separate now for peace. Peace Now," urging the Israeli government to withdraw from the occupied territories in order to achieve peace between the Israelis and the Palestinians.

increasingly fierce opposition to Israel on the part of the Soviet Union and the Soviet Bloc as a whole. Perhaps the lowest point in the history of Zionism was reached on November 10, 1975, when the United Nations General Assembly passed Resolution 3379, determining that "Zionism is a form of racism and racial discrimination." Before the vote was taken, the US ambassador to the UN, Daniel Patrick Moynihan, protested that "the United Nations is about to make anti-Semitism international law.... The United States does not acknowledge, it will not abide by it, will never acquiesce in this infamous act.... A great evil has been loosed upon the world."

It would take sixteen years and, most importantly, the fall of communism in the Soviet Union and Eastern Europe, for this resolution to be rescinded by the United Nations in December 1991. But undoubtedly the most important response to the Yom Kippur War was domestic: the grass-roots distrust in and opposition to the Meir government and that of Rabin that followed it led to an event that was not only unprecedented but in many ways unthinkable: the defeat of the Labor government in the elections of 1977 by the Likud (a new coalition of Herut, the Liberals, and small centrist and right-wing groups).

Much ink has been spilled explaining this victory as a result of a political shift to the right in the Israeli public and especially Begin's appeal to the Jews from former Muslim and Arab states who felt unrepresented and even persecuted by the Ashkenazi Mapai-led elite. While this was to some extent true, there is a much simpler explanation for the Labor defeat and Likud victory: in 1976 a party called the Democratic Movement for Change (DMC) was founded, largely but not exclusively by former Labor Party members and sympathizers who called for fundamental changes in Israeli politics, particularly the introduction of a constitution. In the election of May 17, 1977, the DMC received the third greatest number of seats. After much internal debate, this new party decided to join forces with Likud instead of Labor, and so Menachem Begin became prime minister of Israel.

Ben-Gurion had died in 1973, and so he did not live to see this day that undoubtedly would have caused him the greatest imaginable grief (beyond an Israeli loss in war): a triumphant Revisionist Zionism. Zionism would never be the same again.

Chapter 9
Swing to the right, 1977–1995

When Menachem Begin took office as prime minister of Israel on June 20, 1977, his goal was clear: to implement as quickly and as extensively as possible the policies of Revisionist Zionism as articulated by his mentor and hero, Vladimir Jabotinsky. This meant opposing any territorial concessions that would diminish the gains of the 1967 war; expanding Jewish settlements in "Judea and Samaria"—a.k.a. the Occupied Territories; and transforming the economy of Israel from a Scandinavian-style social welfare model to an American-style capitalist system with as little state interference as possible. Thus, the new minister of finance announced the beginning of an "economic turnaround" that would start with foreign currency liberalization and proceed to transform Israel into a thriving capitalist state, and the prime minister invited to Jerusalem the conservative American economist Milton Friedman, for guidance in economic and fiscal policy.

But five months later, Begin, his government, and indeed the whole world were stunned by an announcement from Cairo: President Anwar Sadat was ready to travel to Jerusalem to negotiate directly for peace with the Israeli government. Ten days later, on November 20, 1977, Sadat arrived at Lod Airport and was met by the president, prime minister, and the cabinet of the state with which he was still at war. He then proceeded to the Knesset, where he gave a speech that offered a full peace treaty with Israel on the condition that Israel withdraw from all the territories it had gained in 1967 and solve the Palestinian problem. It is unlikely that he expected Israel to meet his demands; more likely, he decided that it was in Egypt's best interest for him to engage in direct negotiations with Israel that would not involve the international community and to concentrate on his main goal: the return of the Sinai Peninsula to Egypt. To what extent Sadat personally cared about solving the Palestinian problem is unknown; in the event he was prepared to sign a deal with Israel that would provide some amelioration of the Palestinians' situation under occupation, but without the return of territories in the West Bank, the Golan Heights, and Gaza, not to speak of the right of return of Palestinian refugees.

8. In the fall of 1977, Egyptian president Anwar Sadat visited the Knesset, the Israeli parliament, to attempt to reach a peace treaty with the Jewish state. After intense and difficult negotiations, on March 26, 1979, the two countries signed a peace treaty, which led to Israel's return of the Sinai Peninsula to Egypt and a long-lived peace between the two countries.

Begin would, of course, concede these points, but negotiations did begin, and after months of intense and fractious talks held under the auspices of President Jimmy Carter, Israel and Egypt agreed on September 18, 1978, to the Camp David Accords, which promised the return of the Sinai Peninsula to Egypt in exchange for a full peace treaty between the two countries, and a vaguely outlined plan for national autonomy for the Palestinians that fell far short of independence. After Nobel Peace prizes were awarded to Sadat and Begin, Israel and Egypt signed a formal peace treaty on March 26, 1979. Despite all the revolutionary turmoil in Egypt and the Mideast as a whole, this treaty remains intact.

The crucial fact here is that for Begin, the Sinai Peninsula was not part of greater Israel, and therefore trading it back to Egypt in exchange for peace did not compromise his basic principles. Second, it seems highly likely that Begin based his ideas on Palestinian autonomy on the minority rights treaties after World War I, which made the acquisition of statehood on the part of countries in Eastern, Central, and Southern Europe contingent on their recognizing the national and cultural rights of their minority populations. And it is likely that Begin well knew that these stipulations of national autonomy for minorities did not in the end work out, overwhelmed by the external and internal policies of the states in which they lived.

Thus, a crucial watershed in the history of Zionism occurred: for the first time in the history of the movement, the once marginalized Revisionist version of Zionism came to power in the Jewish state and then presided over the first withdrawal from territory won by Israel in 1967. It is noteworthy that at virtually the same time, the last remaining elder statesman of Labor Zionism died: Golda Meir, aged eighty. It seemed as if the pendulum of Zionism had swung decisively to the right.

But when the next elections were held on June 30, 1981, the country was again divided almost exactly in half. And less than a year later,

Begin's popularity would be assailed on his right, when the fourteen Jewish settlements in the Sinai Peninsula were torn down by the IDF, their population evacuated. For the first time Israelis witnessed the sight of Jewish soldiers and police forcefully removing other Jews from their homes and synagogues, the men often clad in prayer shawls and phylacteries, brandishing Israeli flags.

But the greatest blow to the Begin government and to Revisionist Zionism came only two months later, after Defense Minister Ariel Sharon convinced Begin to invade southern Lebanon in order to defeat the Palestinian forces there that had been shelling Israel from the north and to install a Christian government in power in Lebanon. But Sharon then took one crucial step further, pushing the IDF into Beirut itself. Soon, two large Palestinian refugee camps, Sabra and Shatila, were overwhelmed by Christian armed forces, and a massive massacre occurred in which hundreds (or thousands, depending on which source one accepts) were murdered. For Israel, the military success on the ground was far less than even a Pyrrhic victory: it was abundantly clear that the IDF had not committed the atrocities itself but had stood by and provided cover for the Lebanese Christians to carry out the massacres. Israel, Begin, and Sharon were held responsible for the killings by a good part of the world—including much of the left in Israel, particularly those affiliated with the burgeoning Peace Now movement.

An official government commission headed by a Supreme Court justice was established to investigate the massacres. After long deliberations it exonerated Begin of any responsibility, but held that Sharon, the chief of staff of the IDF, and the head of military intelligence were derelict in their duties for not foreseeing the killings, and they all had to resign. Sharon at first refused to do so, but later gave up the defense ministry and remained a "minister without portfolio" in the government.

Soon, Prime Minister Begin slowly faded into a profound depression that led to his resignation and then his death in 1983.

The election that followed, in July 1984, once more showed that the nation was split in half between right and left. This led to a rotation system for the prime ministership, with Shimon Peres of the Labor Alignment leading a national unity government for the first half of the term and Yitzhak Shamir of Likud for the second half.

Two crucial events in the history of Zionism came to the fore in these elections. First, they witnessed the final demise, almost without a whimper, of Mapam—the Marxist-Zionist party that had been the second most powerful movement in the first elections in Israel, the ideological mainstay of the most rigorous (or doctrinaire) kibbutzim, and the one major Zionist party committed, before 1948, to a binational solution to the problem of Palestine. The Labor Alignment still maintained formal adherence to democratic socialism and hence its membership in the Second International, and flew the red flag over its party headquarters on May Day (until, that is, that practice was eliminated as hundreds of thousands of immigrants came to Israel from the dissolving, and then former, Soviet Union). But in fact "socialism" meant little or nothing to the Israel Labor Party after the death of its old guard, and the ideology of the party was far closer to American liberalism than to any European socialist party (save perhaps the "New Labor" of Tony Blair).

The second watershed in the 1984 elections was the appearance of a new party named "Shas," the Hebrew acronym for *shomrei sefarad*, or Sephardi Guards. This was an Ultra-Orthodox party for Jews of Sephardic and Mizrachi background, which was formed under the tutelage of the Sephardic chief rabbi of Israel, Ovadiah Yosef, and devoted to spreading and protecting its form of Orthodox Judaism while fighting discrimination against non-Ashkenazic Jews in Israel's political, social, and economic life. Like its Ashkenazic parent, the Agudat Yisrael, Shas was not a Zionist party: its non-Zionist ideology rejected the goals of both secular and national religious Zionism. Its goal was for Israel to be governed by Jewish law, as determined by its rabbinate; to educate the children of its community in its own, separate, school system; and to care for the day-to-day needs of its often impoverished community. It had no particular foreign policy, and was willing, again like the Agudah, to collaborate with any government that advanced its religious demands. However, unlike its Ashkenazic parallel, Shas voters were to a large extent not Ultra-Orthodox Jews but Zionists who largely defined themselves as "traditional" in religious practice and who felt disenfranchised due to their ethnic origins.

This was yet another nail in the coffin of the Labor Party's founding ideology: the profound belief that ethnic divisions among Jews in Israel were merely vestiges of Diaspora Judaism that would disappear as Zionism took root and transformed old-world Jews into new secular and socialist Israelis. But if the socialism of the Labor Party was gradually discarded, this did not mean that the party as whole fell to the wayside. On the contrary, Labor began to be defined by its support for withdrawal from the Occupied Territories and a two-state solution to the problem of Israel/Palestine.

In the midst of these debates, yet another milestone in the history of Zionism occurred, counterintuitively during the prime ministership of Yitzhak Shamir. Since 1958, in the absence of a constitution, the Knesset had enacted a series of "Basic Laws" that served as a proto-constitution: on the government, the presidency, the Knesset, Jerusalem, the army, and so on. On March 17, 1992, the Knesset approved yet another basic law, called the Basic Law: Human Dignity and Liberty. Among its provisions were:

1. ...To protect human dignity and liberty, in order to establish in a Basic Law the values of the State of Israel as a Jewish and democratic state.

2. There shall be no violation of the life, body or dignity of any person as such.

3. There shall be no violation of the property of a person.

4. All persons are entitled to protection of their life, body and dignity.

5. There shall be no deprivation or restriction of the liberty of a person by imprisonment, arrest, extradition or otherwise.

6. (a) All persons are free to leave Israel.
   (b) Every Israel national has the right of entry into Israel from abroad.

7. (a) All persons have the right to privacy and to intimacy.
   (b) There shall be no entry into the private premises of a person who has not consented thereto.
   (c) No search shall be conducted on the private premises of a person, nor in the body or personal effects.
   (d) There shall be no violation of the confidentiality of conversation, or of the writings or records of a person.

The importance of this basic law to the history of Zionism is crucial, if complex. Zionism, like all nationalist movements, called for the subordination of private to public interests: loyalty to the nation superseded family, clan, place of birth, region, even religion, and in a more abstract way even loyalty to oneself, to one's own individual goals and ideals. Zionism followed this logic: the individual had to subordinate himself or herself to the Zionist cause, as manifested after 1948 in the state, the army, and other national institutions. This focus on the group rather than the individual was refracted in a social reality: there were, of course, social and economic divides in Israeli society, but these were far narrower than in America or other capitalist countries. There was a very small class of the very rich, usually involved in international trade, but they did not flaunt their wealth in public and were by no means the role models for Israeli youth. Those were, instead, fighters in one of the prestigious combat units in the IDF, paratroopers, or after 1967, settlers willing to live in the most Spartan surroundings in the name of Zionism. In this ethos the individual and his or her self-realization were almost entirely subject to demands of the nation.

In this spirit, the first right enumerated in the Declaration of Independence was the primary group right: "the natural right of the Jewish people to be masters of their own fate, like all other nations, in their own sovereign State." Only on the basis of the actualization of that right could the new state "ensure complete equality of social and political rights to all its inhabitants irrespective of religion, race or sex [and] guarantee freedom of religion, conscience, language, education and culture." In this formulation, the rights of freedom of speech, religion, and education proceed from the state, not from any higher or anterior source of authority.

The Basic Law: Human Dignity and Liberty overturned this hierarchy—the ultimate source of authority became the human being himself or herself and her or his human dignity and liberty. The consequent rights of freedom of religion, speech, culture, and the like are phrased not as those of "citizens" or "inhabitants" but as those of each individual "person" qua person.

One more aspect of this basic law was crucial: the statement that this law was meant to enshrine the values of the State of Israel as a "Jewish and democratic state." This wording had been used beforehand in less important legal contexts and seemed self-evident, if not innocuous. But from now that wording—"Jewish and democratic state" would become the constitutionally inscribed definition of the state, and the meaning and relative weight of the terms "Jewish" and "democratic" would become the basis for enormous amounts of political and judicial debates in the decades to come.

To an important extent the Basic Law: Human Dignity and Liberty reflected the influence of American norms and American law on the Israeli legislature and judiciary. In a complex related move, the doctrine and practice of "judicial review" was introduced into the Israeli legal system, whereby the Supreme Court could declare a law passed by the Knesset unconstitutional.

That this was based on the American model was no secret to either the defenders or the opponents of this development in Israeli law. This was just one aspect of a far broader transformation of Israel into an American-style consumer society, with its concomitant set of values that were so different from the founding doctrines of virtually all forms of Zionism, left, center, and right.

Meanwhile, in yet another typical reversal in Israeli politics, in the elections of June 23, 1992, Labor solidly beat Likud—but once more, when one added together all the left and liberal groups on one side and all the right wing and religious parties on the other, the result was a near even split in the Knesset. Therefore, in order to form a government, Rabin, once again the leader of the Labor Party, had to include in his coalition the Ultra-Orthodox Shas Party.

With this legislative majority, however, Rabin was able to enter into one of the most historic events in the history of Israel and Zionism: the signing of the Declaration of Principles on Interim Self-Government Arrangements with the Palestinian Liberation Organization on September 13, 1993. For the first time in history, Israel and the representatives of the Palestinian nation agreed that "it is time to put an end to decades of confrontation and conflict, recognize their mutual legitimate and political rights, and strive to live in peaceful coexistence and mutual dignity and security and achieve a just, lasting and comprehensive peace settlement and historic reconciliation through the agreed political process."

The world watched as this agreement—later informally called "Oslo 1"—was signed by Prime Minister Rabin and Chairman Yasser Arafat at the White House, with President Bill Clinton looking on in undisguised glee. A hugely dramatic moment occurred when Arafat held out his hand to shake Rabin's and the Israeli prime minister visibly hesitated for a second, as if to punctuate the fact that he, a former chief of staff of the IDF and

9. Israeli prime minister Yitzhak Rabin (left) and Palestine Liberation Organization chairman Yasser Arafat (right) shake hands in front of US president Bill Clinton after signing the Declaration of Principles on Interim Self-Government Arrangements in September 1993. They agreed to recognize one another, cease hostilities, and create the Palestinian Authority, which would have control over territory then held by Israel.

sworn opponent of Palestinian terror, was now accepting Arafat as an equal "partner in peace." But after that briefest of pauses, Rabin accepted Arafat's hand, and it seemed that the goal of peace between Israel and the Palestinians was nigh.

Immediately, however, the right in Israel shifted into high gear to protest these accords in the strongest possible terms. Political debate in the Zionist movement and then in Israel had always been intense, personal, even vituperative. But now the level of political discourse descended to its lowest levels ever, as massive demonstrations, attended by the leaders of Likud and other parties, condemned Rabin as a traitor, held up pictures of him dressed in Arafat's uniform, and demanded his removal from office. Orthodox and Ultra-Orthodox rabbis began to debate whether the laws of traditional Judaism regarding capital punishment for "informers" or "traitors" were applicable in this case. Israeli society was riven as never before.

And then the unimaginable happened: at a massive peace rally held in the central square of Tel Aviv on the evening of November 4, 1995, Yitzhak Rabin was assassinated by Yigal Amir, a twenty-five-year-old member of the ultra-right-wing religious Zionist movement. The future of the peace process, and, more fundamentally, the state of Israel and the Zionist movement, hung in the balance.

Chapter 10
Transformations of Zionism since 1995

Israel mourned as it never had before. The very idea that a Jew could kill another Jew in cold blood—much less an elected prime minister of the Jewish state—shocked the body politic of Israel and of world Jewry. Thousands thronged the square, later renamed Rabin Square, with flowers, candles, songs, and prayers, both religious and secular. Right-wing politicians publicly regretted the degree of venom that had characterized the demonstrations against Oslo. Orthodox rabbis rethought decisions that called for the death penalty for those who proposed giving back territory to the Arabs; their writings and musings had been only theoretical, they maintained—they absolutely did not condone any violence, much less assassination.

One some level, Rabin's funeral attested to the "new normal" in Israel's foreign standing: both President Mubarak of Egypt and King Hussein of Jordan (with whom Rabin had signed a peace treaty in October 1994) traveled to Jerusalem and eulogized the slain prime minister as a close friend and a man of peace. The two countries that had been the most powerful opponents of Israel in the wars of 1948, 1956, 1967, and 1973 were now at peace with the Jewish state, whose legitimacy and security they acknowledged in law and in life. Was this not an emblem of one of the fundamental goals of Zionism from the start, the "normalization" of the Jewish people?

Perhaps; but as the months passed after Rabin's death, Israel returned to its usual politics, and it soon became clear that Rabin's successor, Shimon Peres, did not command the support of the country. In the elections of May 1996 the Labor Party received only two more seats than Likud. Peres attempted to forge a coalition but could not do so, yielding to the younger and far more conservative Benjamin Netanyahu as prime minister. In due course, Netanyahu would lose the prime ministership to Labor's Ehud Barak and then the leadership of Likud to Ariel Sharon, who became prime minister in 2001.

But soon Likud seemed headed for the political graveyard when Prime Minister Sharon decided, in 2003, to abandon his erstwhile political home to form the new, centrist Kadima (Forward) Party. Its mission was to garner enough support to carry out a unilateral withdrawal from the Gaza Strip, including the destruction of twenty-one Jewish settlements there and several more in the northern West Bank. But Sharon's Kadima Party, too, was short-lived: it won the largest number of seats in the elections of 2006 and 2009 but was soon reduced to a small splinter party that dribbled out to insignificance in later elections.

The second phenomenon that became apparent first in these years was the rise of political parties led and supported by immigrants from the Soviet Union. The emigration of Soviet Jews to Israel all but dried up in 1980 after the Soviet invasion of Afghanistan and the consequent deterioration of American-Soviet relations. But in the mid- and late 1980s, Mikhail Gorbachev's policy of opening up the country and radically restructuring it included allowing a truly massive movement of Jews (and their relatives) to Israel: from 1989 to 2011, roughly 1.25 million immigrants came to Israel from the Soviet Union and its successor states. Together with the nearly three hundred thousand Soviet Jews who had come earlier, this resulted in a population of over a million and a half people—by far the largest migration to Israel from a single country since its founding.

But this migration differed significantly from all other mass migrations to Israel, for the simple reason that about a third of the migrants were not Jews according to traditional Jewish matrilineal law. Their arrival in Israel resulted from the 1970 amendment to the Law of Return that permitted not only Jews to come to the Promised Land but "the child and a grandchild of a Jew, the spouse of a Jew, the spouse of a child of a Jew and the spouse of a grandchild of a Jew, except for a person who has been a Jew and has voluntarily changed his/her religion." Since the rates of Jewish-Gentile intermarriage in the former Soviet Union had been extremely high, a very large number of the immigrants fulfilled the terms of the Law of Return but not those of traditional Jewish law.

This demographic reality led to a new admixture in the history of Zionism. The parties that emerged to represent "Russian" Jews were all right-wing in terms of both foreign and domestic policy: they had viscerally experienced socialism and wanted no part of it in the Jewish state. In foreign policy they were hawkish and right-wing. But on one policy issue they could not compromise: regularizing the status of the massive numbers of non-Jews in their midst. Every week seemed to bring yet another story of a brave soldier killed in the line of battle or an innocent new immigrant killed in a terrorist attack whose mother was not Jewish and who therefore could not be buried in a Jewish cemetery.

Far more broadly, in the absence of civil marriage in Israel, the non-Jewish immigrants to Israel, now proud and loyal citizens of the state, could not marry Jews: their choices were converting to Judaism under the auspices of the Orthodox rabbinate, marrying only other non-Jewish immigrants, or getting married abroad. The new "Russian" parties began to fight for civil marriage in Israel, putting them at loggerheads with their natural political bedfellows, not only the Likud but the increasingly right-wing Orthodox and Ultra-Orthodox. In due course, as the "Russians" became more acclimated to Israel, the Russian parties began to have less influence and power—though their former adherents remained almost to a person on the right wing of Israeli politics.

And indeed soon yet another plank of Ben-Gurion's vision of Zionism fell to the side: the firmly held belief that religion was a thing of the past, that Jews coming to Israel would inevitably be "modernized" and would become, like Ben-Gurion and Jabotinsky (or Rabin and Sharon), secular Jews. While the majority of Jews in Israel remained secular, the "religious sector" grew substantially both in numbers and in power in the decades after the 1973 war. This was to some extent a matter of sheer numbers: in the Ultra-Orthodox community it became common for families to have eight, nine, ten, or more children, and these children married at a far younger age than other Israelis and in turn had the same number of children than their parents, or more. At the same time, it became the norm in these communities that the fathers did not work but studied in Talmudic academies.

Many Ultra-Orthodox women did work outside the home, but given the neglect of secular studies in schools for girls and young women, they lacked many skills necessary for even low-level jobs in the modernizing Israeli economy. As a result, a significant number of Ultra-Orthodox families lived on welfare payments from the government. At the same time, Ultra-Orthodox men did not serve in the military (unlike the Orthodox Zionists.) When Ben-Gurion agreed, before the formation of the state, that men studying in the Ultra-Orthodox yeshivot would be exempt from the draft, there were only several hundred such students; by the turn of the twenty-first century the number had grown to sixty thousand, and these exemptions were strenuously defended at all costs by the Ultra-Orthodox political parties, who most often played a crucial role in the formation of coalition governments.

This resulted in a mounting anger at the fact that the Zionist state was funding and defending non-Zionist Jews, that hard-working secular Israelis were footing the bill for the Ultra-Orthodox, serving in the military, and sometimes losing their lives in defense of those who did not serve. In 1999, a new movement called Shinui (Change) emerged, adamantly opposing state support of religion, rejecting any coalition with religious parties, and calling for abolishing the role of Orthodoxy in the civil life of the state. After some modest gains in the next elections, Shinui disappeared from the Israeli political scene.

In due course, Yair Lapid, the son of the founder of Shinui, formed a new movement pledged to continue his father's legacy. But the younger Lapid's rise and policies reflected the fundamental transformation of Israel in another important sense: the Americanization of its economy. First, the kibbutzim, for decades the arch symbols of socialist Zionism, all but ceased engaging in agriculture in favor of manufacturing, as well as the emerging high-tech industries. This was but a small part of the advance of new and increasingly computer-related technological enterprises in Israel, fueled in part by the large number of immigrants from the former Soviet Union who were trained as engineers. Soon, Israel became a world leader in the high-tech industry, resulting in the appellation "The Start-Up Nation." This new economic reality necessarily led to the growth of a new wealthy and upper middle class in Israeli society, and a huge income inequality emerged between the rich and the poor. And although there were individual wealthy Israelis whose families were of Middle Eastern or North African origin, the vast majority of the super-rich, the merely rich, and the upper middle class were Ashkenazi, and the vast majority of the poor were Arab, Mizrachi, or Ultra-Orthodox. This was a situation that had never even been imagined, much less anticipated, by Zionist ideology. Increasingly, the Ultra-Orthodox parties, both Ashkenazi and Mizrachi, began to present themselves in class as well as religious terms.

On the other side of the economic, political, and cultural spectrum Lapid's party, Yesh Atid—"There is a future"—called for "equalizing the burden," shorthand for requiring Ultra-Orthodox men to serve in the army and dramatically lessening the welfare payments to those families whose parents did not work at productive jobs. Yesh Atid was aggressively and proudly secular, and in the 2013 elections it received the second highest number of seats after Likud. And although the members of this new party were mostly in favor of a two-state solution, Yesh Atid demurred from taking a strong position on the peace process, sticking instead to social and economic policies. But by the next election, the celebrity power of Lapid had waned, and his party dropped significantly in the polls, as the Labor party regained some of its strength.

But the elections of 2013 also witnessed a new development in the history of Zionism as well as the Jewish state: the dramatic rebirth of Orthodox Zionism, and especially of its most right-wing and extremist settler elements. Called Habayit Hayehudi (the Jewish Home) and led by the charismatic American-style millionaire Naftali Bennett, the new party aggressively campaigned for primacy on the extreme right of Israeli politics, espousing a variety of integral nationalism to the right of Netanyahu and openly opposing the two-state solution. The transformation of Orthodox Zionism that had begun in the aftermath of the Six Day War now seemed to have reached its peak. Because of Likud's need to forge a coalition on the right, the Jewish Home held a position of great influence in the government.

But in the next elections, the pendulum swung back in an interesting manner: Likud came first, but the Labor Party (now temporarily renamed the "Zionist Union") regained enough support in the Israeli public to return to second place and thus to be the main opposition to the Netanyahu government.

The pattern repeated time and time again, therefore, persists: both the left, the middle, and the right are riven by splits into smaller parties which therefore inevitably hold the balance of power, while the country as a whole is basically split down the middle on domestic and foreign policies.

Epilogue

"We have not yet lost our hope"

—"Hatikvah" (The Hope), Israeli national anthem

Since its founding in 1897, Zionism was for the most part a matter of merely intramural Jewish interest. Outside the Jewish world little notice was taken of Herzl's founding congress and his attempts at diplomacy with the great powers. Certainly the Balfour Declaration betokened an interest in Zionism in the highest circles of British officialdom, not to speak of the granting of the mandate over Palestine to Great Britain, but this still remained a matter of second-order business for the empire, and much less for world politics as a whole. The Peel Commission of 1936, with its proposal of the partition of Palestine into Jewish and Arab states, is a matter of minor historical importance for anyone but students of Zionism, Israel, and Palestine. Undoubtedly, the Declaration of Independence in 1948 made the front page of newspapers around the globe, but the story of the realization of Zionism in the new state was nowhere so crucial to world affairs as the creation of India and Pakistan a year earlier and the population transfers which ensued, the intensifying Cold War, the Korean conflict, and the launch of Sputnik. Even the Sinai campaign of 1956 paled in comparison to the other conflicts leading to the death throes of the British and French empires.

It was the Six Day War of 1967 that thrust the conflict between Israel, the Arab states, and the Palestinians into the center of world news and attention, with most countries in the West continuing to support the Jewish state. The United Nations vote on the "Zionism is racism" resolution of 1975 presents a clear-cut divide: all the states supporting the measure were either in the Soviet Bloc, had Muslim majorities, or were from the developing world (with the exception of Portugal and Mexico). All states voting against the resolution were European, North American, or South American, plus several African states that had good trade relations with Israel. And contrary to common opinion, support for Israel went up, rather than down, in the decades after that vote: the 1991 vote to rescind the "Zionism is racism" resolution passed with a huge majority: only twenty-six countries, almost all Muslim, were in the opposition. (Relevant here, of course, was the disappearance of the Soviet Union and the Soviet Bloc.) Thus, into the 1990s, the vast majority of Western and developed countries still basically supported the actions of the Israeli state and thus of the "Zionist project," though criticism of the Occupation became more frequent and insistent in Western Europe and among developing countries.

In the late 1990s and into the twenty-first century the conflict between Israel and the Palestinians, and hence over the very meaning and legitimacy of Zionism, thrust itself into the very center of global politics. There is no simple explanation for this development. In the Zionist world the right wing is certain that this is merely a recurrence of anti-Semitism, now masked as anti-Zionism, unfairly scapegoating the Jews, yet again, for the world's sins, and there is indeed substantial evidence that all too often anti-Zionism is indeed used as a mask for anti-Semitism. But most anti-Zionists are not anti-Semites, and the two ideologies cannot be lumped into one. The left insists that it is the Occupation that is at fault for the spread of anti-Israel sentiments and policies: reach a peace treaty with the Palestinians and the opposition to Israel will dissolve.

More narrowly, within world Jewry, the most notable change in regard to Zionism was its movement from the margins of Jewish life to its epicenter. Until 1945, most Orthodox, Reform, and secular Jews around the world were not Zionists; today only a tiny splinter group of the Ultra-Orthodox is anti-Zionist, and the same holds true on the extreme left of the Jewish political spectrum. In between, in the broad mainstream of the Jewish world, support for Zionism and the state of Israel is universal, though serious disputes remain between left, center, and right, and have increased in venom over time.

Beyond basic support for the State of Israel, precisely what Zionism means in the Diaspora in the early twenty-first century is very difficult to assess. Well into the 1960s, there were still active Zionist parties and, importantly, Zionist youth movements throughout the Diaspora, which provided their adherents with a coherent and compelling worldview centered on the ideology of left, right, or centrist Zionism. But everywhere these movements have all but petered out, as the result of the deaths of the older generations and a new sociological reality in which youth groups of any stripe play no significant part in youth culture.

It is an old witticism that in the Diaspora "Zionism means one Jew collecting money from a second Jew to send a third Jew to Israel," and certainly the money keeps on coming, while only a tiny number of North American Jews immigrate to Israel. The most recent figures show that in 2007 American Jews alone contributed $2.1 billion to the Jewish Agency and a large number of NGOs in Israel, and the amount has grown since then, despite the crash of the economy in 2008. In that same year, 2007, the total number of immigrants to Israel from the United States and Canada was 6,643—a tiny proportion of the total Jewish population estimated at 5,649,000.

Beyond money and immigrants, the most obvious manifestation of Zionism on the part of Diaspora Jews comes in the form of lobbying their home governments for support of Israel and its policies. The largest and most famous such group is AIPAC, the American Israel Public Affairs Committee, widely regarded as the most influential lobbying group in the United States after the National Rifle Association. Through the decades, AIPAC's influence on American foreign policy toward Israel has been formidable, if more and more controversial, and has been challenged by groups on the liberal and progressive wings of the political spectrum such as the Israel Policy Forum, the New Israel Fund, and J Street that support Israel but oppose the Occupation. Moreover, AIPAC and its analogues throughout the Diaspora are suffering from the same generational crisis: every poll of Diaspora Jewry reveals that the younger generation of Jews identity far less with Israel and Zionism than their parents and grandparents did. They may support Israel in a very general sense, especially in times of crisis, but Israel as a Jewish state and Zionism as an ideology play a very small role, if any, in their fundamental identities. What this generational shift augurs for the future of Zionism in the Diaspora is unknown.

And certainly the vast majority of Diaspora Jews do not partake in the Zionist movement's most impressive achievement after the creation of a state: the revival of Hebrew as a modern spoken language and the creation of modern Hebrew culture. Whereas in 1870 no one spoke Hebrew as their primary tongue, today there are approximately eight million people who do so with completely unconscious fluency and without any necessary ideological intent: significant numbers of Palestinian Israelis have become bilingual in Hebrew and Arabic, and Ultra-Orthodox Jews who for decades denounced as heretical the use of the Holy Tongue for quotidian concerns have become native speakers of the national language of the state some of them abhor. And in this language there is a remarkably robust culture—literature, music, theater, films, television, the plastic arts, and, more recently, the internet. To take just one example, in 2013 the four major legitimate theaters in Tel Aviv sold 2,202,783 tickets—an enormous number in a metropolitan area with 3,713,200 residents. Many of the plays performed by these troupes contain content that reflects upon Zionism and the crisis in the peace process, but most do not, focusing on the universal themes of theater around the world. To be sure, as in most developed countries, creative artists tend to support left-wing and progressive movements, and Israel is no exception: while there are some artists, singers, authors, playwrights, and so on who espouse right-wing Zionism, the vast majority of the artistic community supports a left-wing version of Zionism, an end to the Occupation, and a two-state solution. The most famous figures of Israeli culture in the last fifty years—Amos Oz, A. B. Yehoshua, David Grossman, Yehuda Amichai, Chava Alberstein, Etgar Keret—all fit into this generalization.

While Zionism's achievement of a state, language, and culture is undeniable, profound questions remain, even beyond the future of the peace process and the occupation, about the viability of secular Zionism in a world that could not be imagined by Herzl or Nordau or Jabotinsky or Ben-Gurion or Begin. To a certain extent the right has responded by adopting some of the rhetoric and symbolism of Orthodoxy, but this feels like awkward "spin" rather than an expression of genuine religious faith. Stopping at the Western Wall before trips abroad might look good as a photo opportunity, but no one is fooled: the same prime ministers who do so do not observe the Sabbath and holidays or the laws of kosher food, not to speak of the rules of what is euphemistically called "family purity"—the laws regarding menstruation and sex.

Indeed, it is an absolutely crucial fact that in the history of Zionism from Herzl to Netanyahu, not one single leader of the movement or prime minister of the state has been a believing and observant Jew: not Herzl, Nordau, Weizmann, Jabotinsky, Ben-Gurion, Sharett, Eshkol, Peres, Shamir, Rabin, Sharon, Barak, Olmert, or Netanyahu; even Begin, who displayed a more respectful stance on religion and observance, was by no means a practicing Jew.

And it is true as well, though largely unknown to most Jews and non-Jews around the world, and often obscured by surveys sponsored by right-wing and Orthodox groups, that the largest group of Jewish citizens of the State of Israel remain secular Zionists, even if they are in tortuous disagreement about what secular Zionism means. The best indices of this phenomenon are not how a person responds to a politicized survey urging him or her to check "traditional" if they have Friday night family dinners or have their sons circumcised but rather which school system they send their children to and which parties they actually vote for in elections. In the 2014–15 school year, for example, almost three times as many Israeli Jewish children attended secular state schools than "state religious" schools—52.2 percent versus 18.5 percent. And in the elections of March 2015, 62.3 percent of Israelis voted for secular Zionist parties, while 16.4 percent cast their ballots for avowedly Orthodox parties.

While there can of course be some crossover in these figures—non-Orthodox parents sending children to Orthodox schools and vice versa, and Orthodox Zionists supporting avowedly secular parties and vice versa, the fundamental reality is that a clear majority of Israeli Jews remain secular, and the most important demographic challenge to the secular majority is not the Orthodox Zionist but the Ultra-Orthodox. In the 2014–15 school year the number of children in the autonomous Ultra-Orthodox schools was 29.3 percent of the total. Thus, the true challenge to secular Zionism in Israel is to respond creatively and in line with democratic principles to the growth and power of the Ultra-Orthodox, most of whom remain steadfastly "non-Zionist" and some virulently anti-Zionist.

Despite these challenges, in the end it is hard not to conclude that in its fundamental twin goals of creating a Jewish state and revolutionizing internal Jewish culture along secular lines in that state, Zionism has succeeded.

And yet. Never in its history has the Zionist movement had to confront the rising opposition to its ideology and to the legitimacy of the state it created that is currently witnessed even in Western countries. The movement to boycott, divest from, and sanction Israel has gained credence in places and among groups formerly thought to be stalwart supporters of the Jewish state, and no one can know how widespread this movement will become in the coming decades if the Occupation continues and the settlements continue to multiply. Unknowable, too, is the extent of the existential dangers to Israel arising in a rapidly destabilizing Middle East.

Thus, the words of "Hatikvah," the anthem of the Zionist movement and then of the State of Israel, still remain an expression of hope rather than of historical certainty: "to be a free nation in our own land, the land of Zion and Jerusalem."

Acknowledgments

I would like to express my gratitude to the Harriman Institute at Columbia University for a generous publication grant; to my doctoral student Gil Rubin for preparing the index and helping with the proofreading; to Nancy Toff at Oxford University Press for her encouragement and patience; and, as usual, to Margie, Ethan, Aaron, and Emma for their love and support.

References

Chapter 1: The Jews: Religion or Nation?

For Isaiah's vision of the messianic era, see Isaiah 2:4 and 11:6.

Chapter 3: Theodor Herzl and the creation of the Zionist movement, 1897–1917

On Herzl's reaction to the Dreyfus affair, see Henry J. Cohen, "Theodor Herzl's Conversion to Zionism," *Jewish Social Studies* 32 (1970): 101–10, and Jacques Kornberg, *Theodor Herzl: From Assimilation to Zionism* (Bloomington: Indiana University Press, 1993).

The Basel Program is available online at: http://www.jewishvirtuallibrary.org/js=ource/Zionism/First_Cong_&_Basel_Program.html.

Chapter 4: The Weizmann era and the Balfour Declaration

For the correspondence between McMahon and Sharif Hussein bin Ali see Office of the Geographer, Bureau of Intelligence and Research, *Jordan-Syria Boundary*, International Boundary Study 94, available online at http://archive.law.fsu.edu/library/collection/LimitsinSeas/IBS094.pdf.

Chapter 6: Zionism in World War II and its aftermath

The original Yiddish poem and a translation into English can be found in Katherine Hellerstein, trans. and ed., *Paper Bridges: Selected*

Poems of Kadya Molodowsky (Detroit: Wayne State University Press, 1999), 352–54.

Chapter 7: Zionism in a Jewish state, 1948–1967

For Rabin's recollections of the expulsions see Yossi Goldstein, *Rabin: Biografiah* (Schocken: Jerusalem, 2006), 63. An excellent new translation of S. Yizhar's *Khirbet Khizeh* by Nicholas De Lange and Yaakob Dweck was published recently (Jerusalem: Ibis, 2008).

For a revisionist view of the so-called status quo agreement see Menachem Friedman, "The Structural Foundation for Religio-Political Accommodation: Fallacy and Reality," in *Israel: The First Decade of Independence*, ed. S. Ilan Troen and Noah Lucas (Albany: State University of New York Press, 1995), 51–81.

The original text of the Law of Return is available online at http://www.jewishagency.org/first-steps/program/5131.

On the Rufeisen/Brother Daniel case, see my "A Jewish Monk? A Legal and Ideological Analysis of the Origins of the 'Who Is a Jew' Controversy in Israel," in *Text and Context: Essays in Modern Jewish History and Historiography in Honor of Ismar Schorsch*, ed. Eli Lederhendler and Jack Wertheimer (New York: Jewish Theological Seminary of America, 2005), 547–77.

Chapter 8: Nationalism and messianism, 1967–1977

The official website of "Jerusalem of Gold" is available at http://www.jerusalemofgold.co.il.

For a critical treatment of the history of the settlements see Gershon Gorenberg, *The Accidental Empire: Israel and the Birth of the Settlements, 1967-1977* (New York: Holt, 2007).

The 1970 amendment to the Law of Return is available online at http://www.jewishagency.org/first-steps/program/5131.

Daniel Patrick Moynihan's speech at the United Nations in opposition to the "Zionism is racism" vote is available online at http://www.unwatch.org/

moynihans-moment-the-historic-1975-u-n-speech-in-response-
to-zionism-is-racism/.

Chapter 9: Swing to the right, 1977–1995

The Basic Law: Human Dignity and Liberty is available online at
https://www.knesset.gov.il/laws/special/eng/basic3_eng.htm.

Further reading

Primary sources

The best anthology of Zionist thought in English remains Arthur
Hertzberg, *The Zionist Idea*, first published in 1959 and released
again in 1997 (Philadelphia: Jewish Publication Society). Its rather
idiosyncratic and very long introduction can be skipped.

Pre-Herzlian Zionist thought is best represented by Leon Pinsker,
Autoemancipation (New York: Zionist Organization of America,
1935), and Ahad Ha'am, *Selected Essays* (New York: Atheneum,
1981).

Crucial are two works by Theodor Herzl, *The Jewish State* (New York:
Dover, 1988) and his utopian novel *Old-New Land* (Princeton, NJ:
M. Wiener, 1997).

The letters of many Zionist leaders have been published; the best of
these are the twenty-five volumes of *The Letters and Papers of
Chaim Weizmann* (London: Oxford University Press, 1968).

There is a dearth of English-language translations of the writings of
Vladimir Jabotinsky; a rather poor but still useful collection is
*Vladimir Jabotinsky, The Political and Social Philosophy of Ze'ev
Jabotinsky*, ed. M. Sarig (Portland, OR: Vallentine Mitchell, 1999).
A far better representative of Jabotinsky's writing is his fascinating
novel *The Five*, ed. and trans. Michael Katz (Ithaca, NY: Cornell
University Press, 2005).

Of great interest is Chaim Weizmann's autobiography *Trial and Error*
(London: Hamish Hamilton, 1949).

Menachem Begin's account of the early years of the State of Israel is
crucial reading: *The Revolt* (New York: Nash, 1977).

General histories of Zionism

The classic *History of Zionism* (New York: Schocken, 2003) by Walter Laqueur merits reading as an insightful if largely outdated text. This is true as well of two volumes by David Vital, *The Origins of Zionism* (Oxford: Oxford University Press, 1975) and *Zionism: The Formative Years* (Oxford: Oxford University Press, 1982).

Two surveys of Zionist thought are useful: Shlomo Avineri, *The Making of Modern Zionism* (New York: Basic Books, 1981), and Gideon Shimoni, *The Zionist Ideology* (Waltham, MA: Brandeis University Press, 1997).

Two short histories of Zionism, Michael Brenner, *Zionism: A Short History* (Princeton, NJ: Markus Wiener, 2011), and David Engel, *Zionism* (Harlow, UK: Pearson/Longman, 2009), parallel this VSI from different perspectives.

The complex story of Zionist ideology regarding the Palestinians is treated in Yosef Gorny, *Zionism and the Arabs* (New York: Oxford University Press, 1987).

General histories of the state of Israel

Howard Sachar, *A History of Israel: From the Rise of Zionism to Our Time* (New York: Knopf, 1976), is now a classic, a factual history of Israel with a great deal of detail regarding Zionist ideology. A more updated and insightful history is Anita Shapira, *Israel* (Waltham, MA: Brandeis University Press, 2012).

Biographies of Zionist thinkers

Steven Zipperstein, *Elusive Prophet: Ahad Ha'am and the Origins of Zionism* (Berkeley: University of California Press, 1993), is an excellent study of this crucial Zionist theoretician.

Of the many biographies of Herzl, the most readable is Amos Elon, *Herzl* (New York: Holt, Rinehart & Winston, 1975). A more critical approach is followed in Ernst Pawel, *The Labyrinth of Exile: A Life of Theodor Herzl* (New York: Farrar Straus & Giroux, 1989). A crucial corrective to the historiography regarding Herzl and the Dreyfus Affair is Jacques Kornberg, *Theodor Herzl: From Assimilation to Zionism* (Bloomington: Indiana University Press, 1993).

The authoritative biography of Chaim Weizmann is Jehuda Reinharz, *Chaim Weizmann: The Making of a Zionist Leader* (New York:

Oxford University Press, 1986) and Reinharz, *Chaim Weizmann: The Making of a Statesman* (New York: Oxford University Press, 1993).

The best guides to Socialist Zionism are Anita Shapira's three excellent biographies of Socialist Zionist leaders: *Berl: The Biography of a Socialist Zionist, Berl Katznelson, 1887–1944* (New York: Oxford University Press, 1984); *Yigal Allon, Native Son: A Biography* (Philadelphia: University of Pennsylvania Press, 2007); and *Ben-Gurion: Father of Modern Israel* (New Haven, CT: Yale University Press, 2014).

There are several biographies of Vladimir Jabotinsky written by his acolytes; the best is Joseph Schechtman's two-volume study: *Vladimir Jabotinsky Story* (New York: T. Yoseloff, 1956–1961). For a different view see my *Zionism and the Fin de Siècle: Cosmopolitanism and Nationalism from Nordau to Jabotinsky* (Berkeley: University of California Press, 2001). On Jabotinsky's leadership of the Revisionist Movement see Jacob Shavit, *Jabotinsky and the Revisionist Movement* (London: Frank Cass, 1988).

A useful study of Jewish Orthodoxy in the early history of Zionism is Ehud Luz, *Parallels Meet* (Philadelphia: Jewish Publication Society, 1988).

Zionism from 1948 to the present

Vital to an understanding of Zionism and Judaism is Aviezer Ravitzky, *Messianism, Zionism, and Jewish Religious Radicalism* (Chicago: University of Chicago Press, 1996). On the emergence of the settlements and settler ideology see Gershon Gorenberg, *The Accidental Empire: Israel and the Birth of the Settlements, 1967–1977* (New York: Times Books, 2006).

The book that led to the rise of the "new historians" phenomenon is Benny Morris, *The Birth of the Palestinian Refugee Problem, 1947–1949* (Cambridge, UK: Cambridge University Press, 1989). On the post-Zionist ideologies see Laurence Silberstein, ed., *Postzionism: A Reader* (New Brunswick, NJ: Rutgers University Press, 2008), and for a more critical view see Anita Shapira and Derek Penslar, eds., *Israeli Historical Revisionism: From Left to Right* (Portland, OR: Frank Cass, 2003).

Index

Zionism

W

Y